Advertising
Policy and Practice

JOHN C. DRIVER
University of Birmingham

GORDON R. FOXALL
Cranfield School of Management

ST. MARTIN'S PRESS   New York

© 1984 The Advertising Association

All rights reserved. For information, write:
St. Martin's Press, Inc., 175 Fifth Avenue, New York, NY 10010
Printed in Great Britain
Phototypesetting by Georgia Origination, Liverpool
First published in the United States of America in 1984

ISBN 0-312-00731-0

Library of Congress Cataloging in Publication Data

Driver, John, 1944–
  Advertising, policy and practice.

  Includes bibliographies and index.
  1. Advertising.   I. Foxall, G. R.   II. Title.
HF5821.D74   1984   659.1   84–40336
ISBN 0-312-00731-0

Contents

Preface

Typically, advertising provokes comment on its features, effects and costs, and speculation about advertisers' intentions and influence; claims abound, accusations are levelled, defences made. Some, on the public's behalf, consider advertising a highly persuasive force which warrants protective measures or the institution of countervailing power. Such a view links advertising with profound effects on the consumer, either through conscious or more complex processes and thus with significant effects on society and the economy. Others, generalising from their own perceptions and behaviour, are more sceptical of its effects and question its value even to advertisers. Advertising often generates intense feeling, relatively little analysis and immoderate conclusions. This book attempts the reverse.

Any approach must necessarily be influenced by what has gone before, but our conception of policy and practice permits the exploration of a variety of theoretical, empirical and administrative issues and thus the conjunction and extension of material in a novel way. Consideration is given to various aspects of advertising management, effects, analysis and regulation, and to several disciplinary perspectives, but we have sought a balance between the pursuit of intellectual refinement for its own sake and the necessary rigour which must underpin the study of advertising. In providing topics of interest for students of economics, business studies and marketing, for practitioners, policy makers and their advisers, commentary is given on, and reference made to, an extensive but often dispersed literature and a variety of arguments presented. The approach is primarily analytical but some more descriptive material which is not readily available elsewhere is also introduced.

The genesis of this book lies in our initial curiosity concerning the inter-relationship of the economics of the Austrian School with the marketing approach to advertising. An initial paper on the Austrian perspective by John Driver was considered by Mike Waterson, Research Director of the Advertising Association, as the basis for a book. Subsequent refinement led to a concept involving policy orientation and a multi-disciplinary perspective in which a variety of approaches not hitherto related are brought together.

With a marketing interest in common the emphasis on economics and consumer psychology has been the more unitary undertaking, but we have benefited from close and sympathetic collaboration throughout the writing of this book and, although initial drafts of all but Chapter 4 were by John Driver, the end result is truly a joint effort in which we share responsibility.

Acknowledgements are due to David Houlcroft and Stephen Littlechild of Birmingham University for comments on an early draft of the Austrian Economics paper, to Philip Circus, Legal Adviser to the Institute of Practitioners in Advertising, who greatly increased the legal precision of Chapter 1 and Appendix 1, to Harold Lind and Duncan Reekie who provided constructive criticism of the final manuscript, and to Mike Waterson who has piloted throughout. Linda Williamson and Margaret Sheridan undertook the typing task with fortitude and cryptographic skill.

John C. Driver
University of Birmingham

Gordon R. Foxall
Cranfield School of Management

March 1984

Introduction

Increasingly books on advertising are prefaced by explanation — sometimes apology — for their adding to an already extensive literature. We readily conform to this convention, at least to the extent of explaining briefly our understanding of the problem to which this book is addressed and our intentions in approaching it.

The span of existing books on aspects of advertising is immense, but whilst certain specialised and generalised needs have been met there appears to be a relative neglect of advertising policy and a partiality in the way it is treated. A variety of forms are adopted but characteristically either policy issues are a concluding adjunct in disciplinary-based approaches and are discussed in that context alone — to the exclusion of a more holistic approach — or the contributions of specific disciplines are ignored in the advocacy of policy change for sectional interest. It is, we believe, indisputable that many disciplinary inputs relate to an understanding of advertising and that such approaches are necessary in providing both a focus for attention, an organised framework for assessment and often the basis for necessary specialisation; however, the combination of knowledge of both policy and practice is essential if disciplinary insights are to contribute.

Therefore, in addressing issues of policy and practice, this book is not concerned with exploiting a narrow uni-disciplinary approach to advertising in general, but with the problem of using knowledge from several disciplines which is relevant to the formulation and execution of public policy on advertising. While recognising that disciplines contribute to policy formulation in a variety of ways, a distinction should be made between the specific contributions of commissioned research and the more general influences that arise from the more abstract discussion of policy. In the latter respect there is often a failure to appreciate the intricacies of policy formulation. Moreover, policy issues are essentially multi-disciplinary and complex. That this is indeed the case with advertising regulatory policy is evident from a recent classification by Boddewyn[1] of twelve forces which shape and therefore define the debate about regulation, based on various rationales — consumer protection, environmentalism, religion and issues arising from technological development and economic change — *each* of which could sustain detailed multi-disciplinary study. So, even restricting policy to the issue of regulation does little to narrow the topic in disciplinary terms.

Increasingly, however, specialisation or at least selectivity is necessary in addressing advertising and this is also the case with advertising policy. The basis of our selection is to draw on those contributions which further the understanding of regulatory policy — from marketing, consumer psychology and economics — but to locate these in a policy-making context, whilst not denying the possibility that disciplines either singly or in combination can elucidate some issues of public policy.

Chapter 1 considers the role of law, the characteristics of the UK self-regulatory system, the measures which have been proposed to modify existing procedures in the light of overseas experience (notably American), and the attempt to achieve harmonisation of EEC regulations. This account briefly examines the philosophical, institutional and administrative contexts in which policy initiatives arise and draws together a widely dispersed literature which has given detailed consideration to the policy issues raised. It should be pointed out, however, that our approach is primarily illustrative so that, for example, in concentrating on print rather than electronic media, a fuller reflection of the underlying issues can be given without the focus on rapid and accelerating technological development that the other would imply. Nevertheless, many of the legislative, semantic and administrative features of policy which have to grapple with the amorphous problems inherent in defining and responding to misleading, false, unfair and manipulative advertising are common to both media and share a disciplinary basis. Also, our focus on what might be termed 'recent history' and 'perennial problems' is not intended to be comprehensive. A specialised treatment is necessary for the various problems posed by the advertising of specific products, certain copy themes, closely-identified target audiences and the unintended recipient. We do not deal with the extensive multi-disciplinary research relating directly to these issues, but examine the premises which do underpin policy in such areas.

In Chapter 2 the economic basis of advertising is discussed and the approaches of economists to advertising policy appraised. The discussion proceeds from the consideration of economic freedoms and the freedom to communicate; these are essentially the historical basis for the evolution of advertising and define its normal context. (This is in contrast to Chapter 1 where the focus is on the pathology of advertising and the moves taken to regulate it.) Paradoxically, much of conventional economic analysis of advertising is often critical even of the existence of advertising and certainly the policy recommendations ensuing from the analysis of information and competition have tended to be restrictive of advertising. In part this follows from inherent limitations in the conception and scope of economics as it relates to the phenomena of advertising but more significantly, it arises from a combination of inappropriate methods of analysis pursued beyond their province. The economic significance of advertising is such that a mismatch between the phenomena of advertising and formal economic analysis is increasingly untenable and to fill this analytical vacuum the alternative approach of the Austrian school of economists is finding increasing attention.

Chapter 3 presents an account and critical appraisal of this method of economic analysis and examines its implications for economic policy. The significance of the methodological individualistic and the subjectivist approach to advertising is contrasted with the aggregative and objective approaches of mainstream economists and, in its underpinning of the positive features, there is some support for alternative policy prescriptions.

The economic analysis of Chapters 2 and 3 rests on a particular conception of the theory of consumer behaviour which traditionally has been based on introspective assumptions and deductive logic rather than on observation of actual behaviour. In the marketing and consumer psychology literatures, different perspectives of consumer behaviour are discussed which lead to other conceptions of the role and significance of advertising. These clearly warrant attention.

Chapter 4 examines the dominant sequential models of consumers' decision processes with their emphasis on information-processing, attitudes and intentions. It contrasts these with the alternative behaviouristic interpretations which are gaining recognition as especially appropriate for the low involvement typically associated with many advertisements and the familiar products to which they relate. In this chapter too the significance of advertising communication is reviewed in the social and marketing contexts in which it operates, and a view taken of how advertising works and its relationship to consumer behaviour. This material is relevant to the economic orientation of the previous chapters in both complementary and contrasting respects. Links arise in the role of information, the degree of deliberation in decision-making, the significance of advertising in communication and in methodological issues concerning the scale and level of enquiry and the scope for generalisation.

Chapter 5 considers the behaviour of producers, including the various contributors to the advertising process within the operating contexts in which decisions are taken and in regard to the available normative theory of how, it is often thought, they ought to behave. The disciplinary input here is primarily from marketing and economics. The producers' utilisation of, if not dependence upon, consumer behaviour research leads to a complementarity with Chapter 4 but, to avoid repetition, the explicit psychological and behavioural science underpinnings of this usage are mainly confined to that chapter. In both cases we have resisted the gravitational pull towards a single disciplinary core which characterises so much work in this area. Chapter 5 also reviews the theory and empirical determination of optimal advertising expenditures and relates this to the practice of advertising definition and budget determination. A marketing view of advertising as a service is adopted including price, distribution channels and the manner in which essential characteristics are emphasised to define the product. Such an approach demonstrates the role of pragmatism in advertising decisions and shows how advertising as communication is part of a competitive process.

The subject matter of this chapter relates to preceding topics in a variety of ways. The consideration of the role of optimisation in advertising decisions is germane to both the traditional and Austrian economic approaches though the subjectivism that is exhibited by advertisers is more in keeping with the latter view, whilst the assumption of objective optimisation implicit in the former approach is, it is argued, of doubtful validity in practice. The nature of advertising competition in marketing, cast in terms of a dynamic process rather than a static state, has affinity to the Austrian view rather than to the traditional microeconomic conception of market structures. Also, in recognition of the heterogeneity of advertising, the fragmentation of audiences and the limitations of knowledge, the scope for entrepreneurship and individualistic decisions is demonstrated.

The various disciplinary approaches and the process of selection exhibited in this book preclude simple summarisation in the concluding chapter. Nevertheless, Chapter 6 draws on the sometimes disparate but often inter-relating influences of earlier discussions and conclusions to complete an overview of how the disciplinary approaches of economics, marketing and psychology contribute to an understanding of advertising practice and policy. Recognising that it is impossible to actually *conclude* a discussion of policy and practice, it is hoped that this book is a *prelude* to an inter-disciplinary synthesis and a contribution to the ongoing debate.

Reference

1.   Boddewyn, J. J., 'Advertising Regulation in the 1980s: The Underlying
     Global Forces', *Journal of Marketing*, Vol. 46, Winter 1982, pp. 27–35.

1

Advertising regulatory policy

1.1 Introduction

Advertisements are a familiar phenomenon and their extent and pervasiveness make them an integral part of both the culture of society and its economy. Indeed the familiarity is such that it is easy to overlook the simple fact that it involves literally millions of communication linkages between advertisements and their recipients, such a figure deriving both from the number of advertisements and the scale of audiences. But it is precisely this familiarity with advertising that challenges the advertiser to make his communication effective and, at the very least, to establish some awareness of his message. In the mass audience the precise effects of any individual advertisement generally remain obscure, though on occasion the advertiser will seek to assess its effectiveness and the recipient may question its effects. However, the low involvement with advertising, the scant attention given to it and the possibly minimal effects deriving from it in general serve to highlight both the acceptance of the phenomenon and to give perspective to the exceptional or exceptionable advertisement or advertising campaign. In the process of striving for that essential recognition and for greater effect an advertisement does on occasions contravene some standard which is then recognised more in the breach than as a result of compliance; otherwise, like good health until it is unsettled, most of advertising may be taken for granted. But what are these standards? From where do they derive? What is their purpose and status? Such questions are our concern in this chapter, where the legal and self-regulatory systems are briefly described and the UK experience is considered in the light of EEC procedures and American comparisons.

1.2 Policy, power and law

Policy is concerned with both the formulation of ends or objectives and the selection and implementation of appropriate means to their attainment. *Public* policy can accordingly be viewed as a concomitant and a privilege of power: without power the means are likely to be ineffectual. However, policy prescriptions are not necessarily defined or articulated in precise terms, especially in the case of matters which are judged to be of comparatively minor importance. Indeed, there is a tendency for the exercise of power to treat these matters only as inclination or immediate events require. Over time their original principles are so modified by a succession of (possibly subtle) adjustments that the precise premises of existing powers may not be readily identifiable. Also, the means adopted for previous purposes, which either are retained or modified in piecemeal fashion, may become increasingly inappropriate. As Lindblom[1] has pointed out, the prevailing view of the formulation and administration of policy casts it as a rational process in which ends are specified and means subsequently sought through a logical and comprehensive search for information about means-ends relationships. In practice, he notes, policy-making usually consists of the simultaneous selection of ends and means since the former often cannot be chosen until the latter are known. Any search for information which is involved in the process of policy reformulation relates to the incremental differences between existing and proposed policies and is thus highly limited. The study of administrative policy-making is most aptly designated 'the science of muddling through' (which is, of course, the title of one of Lindblom's most influential papers, as cited above).

The attempt to unravel the assumed underlying principles of long-term public policy prescriptions and provisions by examining their historical development is, therefore, fraught with difficulty; there may be precious few such principles to be discovered and, in any case, those which are present in the policy formulations and legal instruments governing any given human activity are likely to have evolved gradually, in a somewhat convoluted procedure geared to short-term measures. Nevertheless, in the attempt to determine the nature of contemporary policy, in this case towards advertising, the culmination of most formal deliberation to date is to be found in the exercise of regulatory power enshrined in law. While the 'statement of policy' to be found in legal provisions must be qualified and supplemented by a variety of other influences and institutional considerations, this relatively stable basis from which to view the attempted control of advertising deserves our initial attention. Subsequently the control of advertising through the self-regulatory system will be considered.

The Nature of Advertising Law in the UK

In the UK some 80 statutory laws — Acts of Parliament, Regulations and Orders — are concerned in some way with advertising and a glance at the available list from the British Code of Advertising Practice[2] (Appendix 1), reveals the extraordinary variety of measures which regulate advertising. Certain Acts have both the specific intention and the effect of directly controlling aspects of advertising, whilst others contain implications for advertising which derive incidentally from other, major purposes. This is quite apart from the influence of the common law on advertising and advertising content, for example in respect of the laws of defamation.

Overall the law is concerned with the *physical characteristics* of advertisements, as with posters and signs, and the space and time allocation of advertisements in electronic media. The common law applies, amongst other things, to the means of advertising in private property where trespass or nuisance is involved and in general the provisions of the Town and Country Planning Act (1971) and Regulations (1969) control the nature and extent of outdoor advertising, although Road Traffic Acts and Civil Aviation Acts and Regulations are also applicable, as is the Noise Abatement Act (1960). For electronic media the Broadcasting Act (1981) is the relevant piece of legislation.

The *content* of advertising and the purposes to which it is put are primarily reflected by the Misrepresentation Act (1967), the Trade Descriptions Act (1968) (which prohibits the false or misleading description of goods or false statements about services) and the Fair Trading Act (1973). A number of other provisions deserve a mention: limitations on the reproduction of bank notes, coins and postage stamps, the use of competition, the prevention of defamation, indecency and obscenity, and the passing-off of other trade marks or names all show the variety and extent of advertising control. Also illegal are references to certain diseases or conditions in advertisements to the general public including cancer, TB and VD. The control of content, though having a general effect on all advertisements, does bear more particularly on certain types of product, especially those in the medical or pharmaceutical areas, food, drink and tobacco, and money lending and other financial services. The content of an advertisement must also conform to certain standards imposed by legislation concerned with racial and sexual discrimination.

The general principle that appears to underlie the variety of laws alluded to above is the avoidance of advertisements which deceive or by falsity permit an unfair advantage to be gained over others whether they be fellow advertisers, producers or consumers. Also, advertising itself should not be a nuisance or be detrimental to the well-being of vulnerable groups, especially children and the sick. The means adopted are restriction on certain forms of copy and prohibition of advertising by certain advertisers or in relation to particular products.

Despite the above the comment has nevertheless been made that overall 'there is relatively little formal control of the form and content of advertising'[3] but such a view must be set against an assessment of the adequacy of the law as a means of controlling the form and content of advertising. Such an assessment clearly should consider the detailed provisions of the various Acts and Regulations and the effects they have had on the control of those prescribed practices which ideally should be prevented. But where infringement occurs, the nature of any sanction and form of redress must also be considered. In this case an assessment would also consider the effectiveness of the law in terms of time, effort and cost of its implementation and the certainty of its outcome. Matters which in turn are dependent on the adequacy of definitions of abuse, the means of detection and the efficiency of its enforcement.

Such a comprehensive appraisal of the efficacy of the law is beyond the scope of the present work but a number of points can, nevertheless, be made. It is important initially to distinguish between adverse effects as they variously befall producers and consumers, and to differentiate the direct effects of the advertisement itself from the consequences of behaviour possibly derived from it. These distinctions are important because the impact of advertising abuse may be concentrated and severe in the case of a competitor whose credibility and good standing is compromised, whilst in contrast the impact on an individual advertising recipient may be, objectively, relatively slight. In such cases it is predominantly only the producer who has sufficient cause and adequate incentive to turn to the law. Indeed the thrust of advertising law, both by statute and as a result of case law through litigation, has been directed to the protection of producers and the regulation of advertising standards *vis-à-vis* other advertisers. In part this arose from the development of law relating particularly to advertising, correlated with the growth of the use of advertising and the emergence of mass media, and the extension to advertising of the laws established elsewhere in the regulation of business conduct. This development has been piecemeal and not in accord with any apparent underlying general principles but rather in response to manifest need. But whilst some case law relating to advertising was established, there was reluctance — arising in part from the fear of a 'flood of litigation' and a belief that it was 'not the job of the Courts to try the relative merits of any particular product' — for the courts to involve themselves in the claims of advertisers 'save in extreme cases of malicious falsehood'.[4] Latterly, with a greater reliance by the courts on the establishment of Statute law in accord with the development of political institutions and the principle of democracy, this type of legislation has not been forthcoming in comprehensive form. Rather, it has been part of wider legislation seeking to proscribe, for instance, deceptive practices, as with the Trade Descriptions Act (1968) or, in relation to trademark protection, as with the Trade Marks Act (1938) (see Cornish[5]).

For advertising recipients the consequences of advertising abuse are only occasionally likely to provide sufficient incentive to face the uncertainties and costs of legal remedies, though the effects on a mass audience as a whole of individually slight impacts can warrant some form of collective action. Because of the difficulties in organising such complainants in practical terms, this has been predominantly undertaken by consumer organisations who act as a pool for such grievances and may have the resources and expertise to seek redress. But the consumer interest is better served by the effect the law has in *preventing* abuse thereby removing the difficulties of assessing the scale and variable effects of such abuse and the determination and distribution of any compensation.

There are, however, considerable difficulties in framing legislation to prevent abuse and in setting deterrent penalties commensurate with other offences. It is the likelihood that any such legislation would have some of the following features: low chance of detection and prosecution, non-deterrent penalties, high costs of administration, considerable time lags serving to deter neither the unscrupulous who could positively exploit its inadequacies, nor the unwitting, reckless or careless. This led, at least in the UK, to alternative means of achieving advertising regulation other than the extension of legal provision.

Too much, however, should not be made of the divergent interests of consumers and producers nor of the factors which militate against the efficacy of law. In many cases various Acts do provide protection for both producers and recipients of advertising. These provisions are most marked where whole product categories are protected — where it is illegal to advertise foods and medicines falsely, for instance. But the control of false and misleading statements, including advertising, in the general course of trade are of common benefit to responsible advertisers and consumers. Likewise, there is mutual benefit where unfair and disparaging comparisons are controlled or injurious and unjustified linkages with another's interest are precluded. A major difficulty arises, however, in the distinction between objectively false statements and those which are misleading, incomplete, spurious or otherwise outside the ambit of criminal offences, or insufficiently specific to infringe rights in contract or tort. This, too, is the problem with advertising which offends general moral standards or is merely offensive.

Reformers, presuming that the existing state of advertising is in need of revision, can argue for one of the following alternatives:

1. The extension and development of the law — presumably through statute — to provide a more comprehensive and systematic protection and regulation of the various interests.
2. An extension of the existing procedures to specific products or media.
3. A greater reliance on voluntary codes of practice and self-regulation.

In the absence of comprehensive legislation, the potential benefits are necessarily speculative. Indeed, in the past there has been in the UK a reluctance to follow this route and action has been taken to circumvent its necessity. The operation of the self-regulatory system, to which we turn in the next section, has been the subject of some criticism but under the Fair Trading Act 1973 (Section 124(3)), there is a requirement for the Director General of Fair Trading to encourage Trade Associations to prepare and distribute codes of practice to safeguard consumer interests. These could supplement existing voluntary measures. Moreover, this Act established the Office of Fair Trading, with coercive powers to protect the economic interests of consumers without recourse to the criminal offences and civil law procedures otherwise available to the individual or producers. In addition to economic interests, the Act covers consumers' health, safety and other matters including protection from detrimental or unfair conduct. Through referrals to the Consumer Protection Advisory Committee (now suspended) by the Director General of Fair Trading, and subsequently on his recommendation, the Secretary of State could make an order and impose sanctions to prevent particular practices. One such referral, for instance, led to the prohibition of traders' non-disclosure of their commercial status in classified advertisements.[6]

The overall position of the law regarding the control of advertising in the UK is, however, not entirely central to the detailed and effective regulation of advertising. This task is, broadly speaking, distributed by type of media between television and radio, and other media including newspapers, magazines, posters, bus sides etc., and involves compliance with the various codes laid down. In broadcasting, these are overseen by the Independent Broadcasting Authority (IBA), and entail full scrutiny of advertisements prior to transmission; for other media, the codes are administered by the Advertising Standards Authority (ASA) and the Code of Advertising Practice (CAP) Committee. The operation of the self-regulating system case in the latter respect is now considered in greater detail.

1.3 The self-regulatory system

Traditionally, the advertising industry has operated its own disciplines or standards, backed by the sanction of influencing media to withhold space for offenders. The detailed procedures have varied over time but the present system is traceable to the establishment in 1962 of the Advertising Standards Authority and to the revision of its procedures in the mid-1970s. The organisation of the self-regulatory system has been designed to ensure the independence of its decisions from the pressures arising from advertising or media interests. Thus whilst the system is entirely financed by the advertising industry, through a levy of 0.1% surcharge on gross media rates, there is a separate body, the Advertising Standards Board of Finance (ASBOF) (established 1975) to administer the funds. The Advertising Standards Authority is a company limited by guarantee and its directors are the twelve Council members and the Chairman, who is appointed by ASBOF after consulting the Department of Trade and the Advertising Association. The Chairman must be independent of the advertising business and maintains a majority of independent Council members who are appointed at the sole discretion of the Chairman. (This aspect, amongst others, is analysed by Boddewyn.[7])

The ASA oversees the work of the CAP Committee, which draws up and advises on the British Code of Advertising Practice (BCAP). At present the

CAP Committee is composed of representatives of 20 Trade Associations from the media, advertisers and advertising agencies and, in addition to its formative role in BCAP, it provides a mechanism for the resolution of intra-industry disputes. The sanctions operated by the media are the withholding of an advertiser's space until an offending advertisement is amended or withdrawn, and the deterrent that adverse publicity could arise from citation in the industry case reports of the ASA.

In practice, the ASA and CAP Committee work closely together, with a shared Chief Executive for the respective Secretariats. The CAP Committee is required to keep the ASA informed of its activities, to advise the Council and implement its decisions. Whilst the CAP Committee meets six times a year, there are sub-committees which deal with matters of urgency and with specialised areas of advertising, e.g. financial and mail-order advertising, sales promotion, and health and nutritional claims. The CAP Committee Secretariat provides an information service to advertisers where there are potential difficulties and can require some measure of pre-publication vetting of possibly contentious advertising or of the advertising of those who have previously contravened the Code. The Secretariat administers cases but reference may be made to the Copy Panel which has a prime responsibility on behalf of the CAP Committee for the acceptability of individual advertisements in prospect or on publication. The Copy Panel's decisions are usually taken as final and, although there can be appeal to the CAP Committee and ultimately to the ASA Council, this is unusual.

Unlike the ASA, the CAP Committee does not deal with members of the public and complaints about advertising are either dealt with by the Copy Panel or through the recommendation of the council to the CAP Committee. Each week the ASA Secretariat circulates to Council members details of advertisements where the Code has been broken or where a complaint is not, in its opinion, in breach of the Code. If any member wishes to comment on these cases the matter is referred to the monthly meeting of the Council. The BCAP is reviewed by the CAP Committee and draft amendments are submitted to the ASA. The constitution of the CAP Committee, with appeal to the Council, also provides an adequate mechanism for the regulation of the potentially conflicting interests of different components of the advertising industry, where complaints by competitors approximate 1000 cases a year.

There is scope for abuse amongst those publishers who are not members of the Trade Associations represented on the CAP Committee and for advertisements placed by a publisher in his own medium (which, not being 'paid for space', is not technically subject to the Code). Moreover, whilst the Code ostensibly covers all advertising, including point-of-sale and brochures, the control over sections of this material is less stringent, principally because the sanction of withholding space is unavailable and the possibility of adverse publicity through the ASA may not be sufficient deterrent. Nevertheless, the effectiveness of intra-industry regulation and, more particularly, the effectiveness of control of advertising to protect wider interests obviously depend on the efficacy of the Code itself.

This may be approached from an analysis of the Code's detailed provisions and the standard of advertising co-existent with its operation, where it is necessary to distinguish whether any weaknesses are due to inadequacy of the Code itself or in its implementation. It is preferable that any vetting system should prevent advertisements that contravene the Code from being published, but with an estimated 25 million advertisements[8] in 1977, it is clearly impractical to achieve total effectiveness in this way.* Accordingly, the response to justifiable complaint and the subsequent eradication of abuse is the most important measure of effectiveness available.

The Code imposes basic obligations on the advertiser: to apply the Code in both the spirit and the letter, to ensure that advertisements are 'legal, decent, honest and truthful' and prepared with a sense of responsibility to the consumer, to conform with the principles of fair competition as generally accepted in business, and to ensure that advertising should not be brought into disrepute or public confidence in it reduced.

Adherence to the Code extends the control of advertising beyond that strictly required by law and since the Code applies to all principals and intermediaries in the advertising process, any of whom has a responsibility to ensure compliance with it, the self-vetting process of advertising assessment can potentially occur several times with different people. Whilst this should reduce the incidence of breaches of the Code, there could, perhaps, be errors of omission or indeed wilful disregard of it. Of course the articulation of principles, however laudable, is but a first stage in the establishment of an acceptable form of advertising regulation. The resultant standards of decency, honesty and truthfulness must not only satisfy the regulators themselves, but find a wider acceptance. In this regard the independence of a majority of members of the ASA is crucial since it is ultimately their responsibility to match the regulators' assessment of suitable standards to those prevailing in a changing society. The difficulties in this should not be understated since matters of taste and decency and of the other *subjective* criteria in the Code may, on occasion, permit a variety of interpretations. But whilst the Code attempts a detailed description of its understanding of these matters, the literal interpretation to be expected from the CAP Committee is balanced by the wider concern of the ASA, though their limited capacity to effect changes in the Code might on occasion lead to a mismatch between the standards required and those generally extant. The lack of consultation by the CAP Committee in the formulation of draft revisions to the Code with 'outside' consumer and

---

* Such estimates of the number of advertisements are highly sensitive to the definition of advertising (which is discussed in Chapter 5) and may account for the dramatic disparity between the UK and USA estimates noted later in this Chapter.

producer interests can also impede a current version of the Code from being fully in tune with society's requirements.

In 1978 the Office of Fair Trading (OFT)[9] conducted an assessment of the workings of the self-regulatory system. It noted that the ASA had reviewed in the year to the end of March 1976 some 4269 complaints from the general public and studied in detail those received in November. The breakdown of complaints for the years 1976–77 and 1977–78 is reproduced in Table 1.

In the light of the assessment of the 400 November complaints, the suspicion that the Secretariat's judgement of complaints that were 'unjustified' was likely to be too sympathetic to the advertising industry proved unfounded:

'We were impressed by the Secretariat's decisions, which, with the exception of literally one or two which seemed unduly to favour the advertiser, appeared to be eminently reasonable. We were also impressed by the ability of some members of the public to concoct a complaint with no basis whatsoever.'[10]

The analysis of the complaints procedure led the report to criticise the time periods involved. Although some two-thirds of the (unspecified number of November) complaints upheld resulted in advertisers' reacting to the ASA's request for substantiation by amending or discontinuing the advertisement,[11] the time taken to do this and the lapse of time in general before offending advertisements were denied space or otherwise withdrawn was 'excessive':

'Such delays enable determined advertisers to continue dubious campaigns for far too long; and hold up the checks which are made on undertakings to amend or discontinue advertisements.'[12]

The delays referred to arise from the time taken for the ASA Secretariat to process a complaint and (possibly) to request substantiation from the advertiser, his time of reply, subsequent consideration and the production of a draft conclusion for the advertiser's comment and a subsequent Council decision, which would cumulate to involve delays of several months, though the majority of cases probably take between one and two months.[13]

The goal of eliminating all contraventions of the Code must be seen as unrealistic. In practice there are a range of factors which inevitably contribute to a shortfall. Thus, for example, the scale and complexity of advertising communication necessarily involves many people with their various abilities and motivations in the *interpretation* of the Code, and opinion and judgements will differ. But what is the extent of contravention of the Code? A definitive answer cannot be given but some impression of both the quantitative and qualitative dimensions is possible.

Analysis of complaints whilst providing valuable information does not, however, indicate the extent of contravention of the Code. Offending advertisements may not be recorded by the ASA for a variety of reasons, including ignorance of the Code and the complaints procedure and where communication is with Trading Standards Officers or other bodies. To form an

Table 1   *Analysis of Complaints received by the ASA in 1976/7 and 1977/8*

Complaints	April '76 to March '77		April '77 to March '78	
	Number	%*	Number	%*
Complaints RECEIVED	3850		4269	
Complaints PURSUED referring to:				
mail order delays	627	16	544	13
advertisement content	1304	34	933	22
	1931	50	1477	35
Complaints NOT PURSUED because:				
concerned with broadcasts	156	4	277	6
outside ASA remit	438	11	591	14
considered unjustified	728	19	925	22
already investigated	412	11	720	17
insufficient information	185	5	279	6
	1919	50	2792	65
	3850	100	4269	100

* %'s rounded

Source: Adapted from 'Review of UK Self-Regulatory System of Advertising Control', Office of Fair Trading, 1978, p. 9.

estimate of the proportion of advertisements in breach of the Code in newspapers and magazines, the Office of Fair Trading commissioned research (for details see Chapter 3 of the above cited report) which examined a sample of 2993 advertisements in March 1978. The results indicated high compliance with the Code: 7 per cent overall were judged to 'fail' but national as opposed to regional publications had a 'success rate' of 87–94 per cent. The report concluded:

'But few of the infringements seem to us to amount to gross deception likely to cause consumers significant harm.'[14]

Other indicators of the degree of contravention of the Code are the numbers of adverse reports circulated by the ASA in its monthly Case Reports and the frequency of space-withholding from offending advertisers. These indicators are compared with the complaints figures in Table 2 below.

On the basis of its analysis of the workings of the self-regulatory system, the OFT made a number of recommendations. A number of these are minor or are concerned primarily with the detail of the operation and involve no matters of principle. (The recommendations are: that the Code should be more effective over all non-broadcast advertising; that Council members should be appointed after wider consultation; that the Council should be expanded to lighten members' work loads and otherwise to expedite business; that CAP Committee intra-industry complaints should be published in the ASA monthly case reports; that foreign language advertisements and 'free' space advertising should be covered by the Code; that stop orders should go to individual publishers; that postal decisions should be instituted by the ASA. There is also a recommendation for an extension of the vetting and monitoring work of the Secretariat.) More significantly, the report recommended an extension of powers in two principal directions:

1. Consideration should be given to a system of fines and corrective advertising under the self-regulatory system.

Table 2   Complaints pursued and Action Taken by the ASA in 1976/77 and 1977/78

	1976/77		1977/78	
No. of complaints pursued	1931		1947	
No. of space 'stops' (advertisers of)				
mail order	(29)	50	(32)	72
content		33		18
ASA monthly report citations	530		447	

Source: As Table 1 and data from Chapter 5 thereof, pp. 38 and 39.

2. (most significantly of all) New *statutory* powers should be available. These
    would not be needed to meet an existing situation of widespread abuse of
    advertising and major deficiencies in the self-regulatory system, but rather
    they would be reserve powers to supplement and strengthen the self-
    regulatory system and to achieve a wider compliance with the Code.

The Director General of Fair Trading, however, did not favour the
conversion of the ASA into a statutory body with statutory powers since this
'would be likely to weaken the industry's commit ment to maintain and finance
self-regulation,'[15] would lead to a legalistic approach with breaches of the spirit
of the code and in practice might be less responsive to the public interest. The
recommendation is for a government body to have statutory powers to enforce
the Code. The report envisaged the Director General of Fair Trading having the
power to apply to the High Court for an injunction to restrain the advertiser or
the publisher of an advertisement 'likely to deceive, mislead or confuse with
regard to any material fact,' or where, in the opinion of the Director General of
Fair Trading, 'speedy and effective action was required to prevent the
continued use of the advertisement', where the ASA had been or was likely to
be ineffective in preventing it.

Before turning to the reception that the review and recommendations
concerning the self-regulatory system was accorded, it is necessary to recognise
additional influences that coincided with the Director General of Fair Trading's
study in the late 1970s. In March 1978, the EEC Commission presented a
draft Directive to the Council of Ministers concerning misleading and unfair
advertising[16] and, as a result of a critical speech in September 1978 made by the
then Secretary of State for Prices and Consumer Protection,* the advertising
industry was invited to consider how some deficiencies of the self-regulatory
system could be eliminated. Subsequently, a working party was set up in
February 1979, comprising a membership from the Advertising Association,
the ASA, National Consumer Council, OFT, Home Office, Lord Chancellor's
Department, and the Department of Prices and Consumer Protection, under
the chairmanship of an official of the last-named department. The accepted
terms of reference adopted by this working party were:

'To consider how best to reinforce the existing self-regulatory system of
advertising control in the United Kingdom by the addition of some new
statutory powers; to recommend particular legislative proposals and to
report.'[17]

These terms presumed the necessity for some statutory reinforcement, but
following a change of government in May and administrative reorganisation
the Working Party proceeded with amended terms of reference in July 1979:

'To consider whether, and if so to what extent, the existing self-regulatory

---

* See *The Times* 26 September 1978.

system of advertising control in the United Kingdom requires reinforcement; to make necessary recommendations and to report.'[18]

Effectively, the Parliamentary scrutineers of the EEC's draft Directive and the Working Party were considering broadly the same issues with indeed some overlap of representative organisations. The coincidence of these deliberations was not exact, however, and subsequent discussion here follows the discussion of the draft Directive by the Select Committee on the European Communities, which preceded the Working Party's report.

The EEC draft Directive concerning misleading advertisements

The purpose of the Directive (Appendix 2) is to ensure the approximation of the laws, regulations and administrative provisions of the Member States, in respect of misleading and unfair advertising. The move to harmonise procedures from different bases in various countries obviously has different implications for the various States; however, the discussion here relates primarily to the UK.

It must be noted at the outset that the Directive raises broader questions than those raised by the previous analysis of the UK self-regulatory system. Subsequently, it will be necessary to view this wider context and the disciplinary considerations illustrating the role and effects — particularly of competition — that are the fundamental underpinnings of the Directive. Also, to provide a comparison with the proposed legalistic approach of the Directive, the relevant experience in the USA will be discussed. Immediately, however, the Directive is considered in some detail.

The *premises* of the Directive provide a definitive context in which misleading and unfair advertising is considered a problem. The major points are that advertising has a 'direct effect on the establishment and the functioning of the common market', and that 'unfair and misleading advertising is likely to restrict the establishment of a system to ensure that competition is not distorted'. The consumer acting on such advertising is inadequately protected. The benefits of harmonisation of provisions against such advertising is in the interest of the public in general and of consumers and competitors; harmonisation would lead to the implementation of advertising campaigns beyond national boundaries and thus affect the free circulation of goods and services. Discussion of the nature and definition of advertising that may be considered misleading and unfair, and the extent of the methods to deal with it complete the preamble. Thus some forms of communication, e.g. policy statements and the publication of comparative product tests by independent organisations would be explicitly excluded but otherwise advertising is to be defined 'broadly', and 'unfair' and 'misleading' must be defined as far as possible by reference to 'objective criteria'. Comparative advertising may be beneficial to the extent that it compares material and verifiable details. The burden of proof for any factual claim made by an advertiser must lie with him. The law — whether civil, administrative or criminal, or a combination — must be adequate and effective; persons and associations must have facilities to initiate proceedings and to obtain quick correction of misleading and unfair advertising. The law should not preclude the adoption of other measures in accord with Treaty of Rome obligations toward the free movement of goods and services, and competition.

In the ten Articles of the draft Directive, 'advertising' is 'any pronouncement for the purpose of promoting the supply of goods and services', 'misleading advertising' means 'any advertising which is entirely or partially false or which, having regard to its total effect, including its presentation, misleads or is likely to mislead persons addressed or reached thereby, unless it could not reasonably be foreseen that these persons would be reached thereby'. Misleading can occur through omission of material information which 'gives a false impression or arouses expectations which the advertiser cannot satisfy'. 'Unfair advertising' is that which 'casts discredit on another person by improper reference', injures reputation and defrauds, 'appeals to sentiments of fear or promotes social or religious discrimination', discriminates between the sexes in social, economic or cultural terms, 'exploits the trust, credulity or lack of experience of a consumer' or has improper influence over consumers or the public.

Advertising should be considered against the characteristics and properties of the goods and services, and the identity and attributes of the advertiser. The courts must be enabled to order the 'prohibition or cessation of misleading or unfair advertising' and 'to take such a decision under an accelerated procedure, with an interim or final effect' . . . 'even without proof of fault or of actual prejudice' and to order publication of a corrective statement and the court's decision in an adequate form, at their discretion. The sanctions would be a deterrent to the infringement of these laws and would 'where appropriate, take into account the financial outlay on the advertising, the extent of the damage and any profit resulting from the advertising'. The right of persons or associates with a legitimate interest to initiate proceedings through the courts carries an associated right to refer the matter to any self-regulatory bodies. Compliance with the Directive was required within 18 months of its notification.

In the UK, an initial official consideration of the draft Directive was conducted by the Select Committee on the European Communities of the House of Lords and subsequently by the Select Committee on European Legislation of the House of Commons.[19] The House of Lords Committee received extensive written and oral evidence from a variety of organisations reflecting the interests in advertising, including the Advertising Association, the ASA, the National Consumer Council, the Consumers' Association, the Incorporated Society of British Advertisers, the Mail-Order Publishers' Authority, the Finance Houses' Association, and the British Bankers' Association. Its conclusions were wide-ranging over matters of detail and principle. They favoured deletion of the Directive's provisions on unfair advertising on the grounds of imprecision and redundancy; although the term 'improper' is used both in connection with reference to nationality, origin, private life or good name and with advertising's power to 'influence' the consumer or the public in general, it is not further defined and in the Committee's view this would give too much discretion to the courts. Furthermore, the provisions on libel and slander were already incorporated in law.

The Committee's reservations on the drafting of the Directive are more extensive, however; for instance, on 'misleading advertising' the materiality of the degree of 'misleading' is unspecified, as is the precise nature of 'material information' that might be omitted from an advertisement, thus rendering it misleading on this count. The culpable person, the 'advertiser' is not defined either. Thus it is uncertain whether the law is to apply to principal or agent or indeed publishers and printers also, so some defence for innocent members of the chain of advertising should be incorporated on the grounds perhaps of accident or mistake, along the lines generally provided for by UK laws. On matters of procedure the Committee concluded that:

'The special court procedure provided for in the Draft Directive should not be accepted, since it cannot be made to fit into the existing systems of the United Kingdom, and represents an attempt to replace our existing method of preventing misleading advertising which is consonant with our current legal system and which, on the evidence, appears to be more efficient than those of other Member States.'[20]

The particular difficulties arising from the Directive lie: in the novelty of the procedures whereby an 'association' would be able to bring proceedings; in that the power to issue publication of a corrective statement is 'hitherto unknown'; in that the burden of proof of the correctness of a factual statement would be on the defendant rather than on the prosecution as is normal in criminal cases; in that a *prima facie* case that an advertisement is untrue would not even be required. In the Committee's view the UK's self-regulatory system, despite some loopholes, is 'efficient and economical' and 'it would be unwise to set up alongside it the legal system called for by the Directive which might supplant the self-regulatory system, and not work so well'. Specifically, the legal system would be slower and subject to appeals, and would not be preventive except through deterrence. Finally, the Committee challenged the premises and legitimacy of the Directive. It could find no evidence that the different degrees of legal protection in the EEC affected the functioning of the market, as required under Article 189 of the Treaty, and that the Directive itself was *ultra vires* because under Article 189 a Directive can be binding as to the 'result to be achieved' . . . 'but shall leave to the national authorities the choice of form and methods' whereas this Directive proposed both the objective and the means.

The House of Commons Select Committee on European Legislation concurred with the House of Lords Select Committee recommendation that the draft Directive raised important matters of policy and principle (in line with the conclusions above), and drew particular attention to three aspects of the special court procedure:

'(i)   the requirement that associations as well as individuals should be allowed to institute proceedings,

(ii)   the provision of the granting of injunctions without proof of fault on the part of the advertiser or actual loss or damage caused to the plaintiff,

(iii) the responsibility laid on the courts to settle the terms of a corrective statement for publication. The Committee are advised that if implemented these would represent significant innovations in United Kingdom law and practice.'[21]

The Commission's draft Directive was subsequently amended[22] (Appendix 3) in the light of opinions of the European Parliament and the Economic and Social Committee, and re-submitted to the Council of Ministers in July 1979 with a requirement that it should be implemented within 24 months of its notification. This amended draft was considered by the House of Lords Select Committee,[23] which found that most of its original criticisms had not been met; the Directive was not *intra vires* in its opinion, nor was the amended draft Directive conducive to the maintenance of the United Kingdom self-regulatory system.

It should be briefly noted that a revised definition of 'advertising' is given but not of an 'advertiser' leaving the location of any culpability unspecific. The word 'improper' is deleted in one clause in the definition of 'unfair advertising' but is retained in another. The use of the words 'appeals to sentiments of fear' and 'exploits the trust, credulity or lack of experience of a consumer' is amended to 'abuses or unjustifiably arouses sentiments of fear' and 'abuses the trust . . . ' but changing 'exploits' to 'abuses' does not adequately define what the standard of impropriety would be, nor the standard of intelligence expected of the consumer. The provision that misleading can occur through the omission of material information remains, with 'material information' undefined. But the amendment refers to the arousal of 'reasonable' (rather than 'any') expectations as a basis for misleading.

The amended draft is more significantly modified in the procedures for enforcement. There is a proposed introduction of 'an administrative authority with adequate powers' as an alternative to legal proceedings against misleading and unfair advertising. This authority, however, could be reviewed by the courts at the request of a party who alleges 'improper exercise' or 'failure to exercise its powers or to apply reasonable standards'. Although the European Parliament had intended that the amendment to include an administrative authority was to 'recognise the effectiveness of the self-regulating system of advertising control in the United Kingdom', the amendment's wording was such as to 'not allow the ASA to continue to regulate advertising in the UK', at least in the opinion of the Department of Trade.[24] Moreover, the financing of the ASA via the ASBOF, with the power of the advertising industry to withhold financial support, makes the ASA's compliance with the provision that 'the authority shall not be controlled by advertising interests' subject to some doubt. In addition, the ASA would not have the powers to order the 'prohibition or cessation of misleading or unfair advertising'.

In regard to the burden of proof of an advertiser's claim, the amended draft effectively placed this with the prosecution in criminal cases, but maintained the onus on the advertiser in civil and administrative cases. Also, cases could be brought 'even without proof of intention or negligence or of actual prejudice' arising from misleading or unfair advertising.

In conclusion, the Committee noted that:

'The Commission have done little to solve the problems raised by the Committee in their previous Report . . . . The Committee feel strongly that the proposal should be amended so that the existing self-regulatory controls may be maintained.'

At the time of writing there have been no further developments to report.

Report of the working party on the self-regulatory system

Following the report of the Director General of Fair Trading on the self-regulatory system, the moves of the EEC for a more comprehensive legal approach to the control of advertising and the views taken by the Select Committee of both Houses, the Working Party sought means which were in accord with the Directive's objectives, yet more compatible with existing United Kingdom law and practice. The identified weaknesses of the existing self-regulatory system were that not all non-broadcast advertising was covered, the ASA's sanctions required compliance by advertiser and/or media which could be flouted and there was no means of securing immediate preventive action against major perpetrators of misleading advertising. The four options considered by the Working Party as remedies, and their outcomes, were as follows:[25]

1. Statutory recognition of Codes of Practice would entail revision to make breaches sufficiently clear as to be amenable to legal processes. This would both compromise the voluntary aspect of the Code and make it less easy to change, it would encourage compliance with the letter rather than the spirit of the code and, whilst it might be a means of making the Code binding on current non-subscribers to the self-regulatory arrangements, the risk of undermining the existing system with its known benefits was not favoured.
2. The option of extending the Trade Descriptions Act 1968 to give the Code legal backing was rejected on the grounds that the terms of the Code were

too general and not appropriate in criminal law; besides, the over-loading of the courts and the low priority hitherto accorded to prosecutions under this Act made the prospect of speedy support for self-regulatory arrangements uncertain.

3. The third option considered was the institution of a duty on the advertising industry 'not to publish an advertisement which was likely to deceive or mislead with regard to any material fact'. The Director General of Fair Trading could then apply for an injunction where an advertisement in his opinion breached this duty, with non-compliance being a contempt of court usually punishable by a fine. This procedure would be applicable to all advertisers and so reinforce the self-regulatory system — and it would be speedy. But to obtain an interim injunction the Director General of Fair Trading would have to convince the court that benefit to the public was greater than the loss to the advertiser. This would be uncertain, but the prospect of an injunction and attendant adverse publicity would be a deterrent and encourage compliance both with the Code and the duty not to mislead or deceive. Furthermore, Part III of the Fair Trading Act would enable the Director General of Fair Trading to obtain assurances from persistent offenders that they would henceforth desist.

4. Similar in effect to injunctions, and stemming from the creation of the same general duty, would be the procedure whereby the Director General of Fair Trading would issue a prohibition order — prohibiting the publication of an advertisement — in cases where the general detriment was greater than the advertiser's loss. This would be equally speedy and effective, but subject to appeal and possibly it would be more arbitrarily imposed; it would also be less consistent with the self-regulatory system.

Accordingly, the Working Party favoured the injunctive procedures from these four options. It should be noted, however, that the advertising industry representation in the Working Party was not convinced of the need for legal reinforcement of the Code.

Additional improvements to the self-regulatory system would arise if the ASA were to extend its publicity of important violations of the Code, institute corrective action including direct corrective statements to individuals misled, encourage further use of vetting of advertisements and the wider use of disclaimers and disclosures to enhance consumer information. The Working Party thought there was scope, with the co-operation of appropriate associations, for some system of fines within Trade Associations and for redress for individual consumers through some sort of conciliation and arbitration scheme.

1.4 The American experience

The American experience provides an example of a more comprehensive legal approach to advertising control and certain similarities in objectives, definitions and methods of American procedures can be seen in the EEC Directive. There are, of course, many differences of content, institutions and philosophy which a thoroughgoing comparison would need to explore. Here, some of the salient features of the American system and its workings are briefly described.

Advertising regulation in the United States is administered by the powers vested in the Federal Trade Commission (FTC) which also has responsibilities in areas unconnected with advertising. The impetus to control advertising arose from a wider concern to control deception, which was a matter for the FTC's interest in such cases as the enticement of competitors' employees, industrial espionage, and the misleading description of goods where the prevailing concern was the effects of description under the interpretation of 'unfair methods of competition' in Section 5 of the Federal Trade Commission Act 1914. In regard to advertising false claims, there was concern amongst producers of specific product classes that the behaviour of wrong-doers, whilst having some adverse effects on consumers, was inimical to the interests of responsible producers and, accordingly, Trade Associations sought the FTC's assistance to enforce their codes. But, in addition, a plethora of small producers complained of the actions of other local competitors. One of the more significant cases in the 1930s led to legislative changes. Thus, in 1931, at the behest of the American Medical Association, the FTC issued a 'cease and desist' order, on the basis of counter medical evidence alone, against the Raladam Company's 'scientific' claims for a patent medicine which supposedly reduced obesity. This order was subsequently set aside by the Court of Appeals and the Supreme Court on the grounds that no harm to competitive interests had been shown at the original trial. Although such detriment to competitors as a result of Raladam's misleading and deceptive statements was subsequently demonstrated in another case brought by the FTC in 1935, there was concern that the FTC should be empowered to protect the interests of the general public as well as those of competitive interests. Accordingly, in 1935, the FTC recommended new legislation which, in the Wheeler Lea Act 1938, amended the 1914 Act thus:

'Unfair methods of competition in commerce, and unfair or deceptive acts or practices in commerce are hereby declared unlawful.'

The intent behind this change is clear from a House Report:

'Reasonable latitude must be conceded to the salesman and advertiser in boosting his own purpose. It is not the purpose of the committee to ignore the realities of this situation. On the other hand, we cannot ignore the evils and abuses of advertising; the imposition upon the unsuspecting; and the downright criminality of preying upon the sick as well as the consuming public through fraudulent, false or subtle misleading advertisements.'[26]

The principal method available to the FTC from the 1914 Act was the power of the 'cease and desist' order to which reference has been made above. Such an order could be issued only after an initial complaint stating the FTC's charges had been served, an opportunity given for a hearing, and the subsequent writing of a report on the FTC's findings. The effectiveness of this sanction in the control of abuses of advertising was limited in a variety of respects. In the crucial field of detection of offending advertising, the resources of the FTC were generally conceded to be inadequate to the task of vetting advertisements; indeed, the sheer number of advertisements would have provided a daunting problem even for an enormous staff. An estimate made in 1967 of the volume of advertisements in the US *per day* put it at 4.2 *billion*.[27] In practice, the general advertising recipient had little incentive to complain and may have been ignorant of the means so to do, or unable to present a sufficiently informed complaint. On the other hand, an aggrieved competitor had considerable incentive and the expertise: attention could be concentrated on only competitors' advertising and familiarity with the product field enabled deceptive claims to be detected. Moreover, since the FTC shouldered the litigation expenses that otherwise would have been carried by the complainant, there was an additional incentive to complain, whilst the defendant was forced to bear his costs in the proceedings and thereby had his competitive costs increased by this tactic.[28] The effects of this were likely to be greater for smaller companies and lesser advertisers rather than the giant firms and there was a widespread belief that the FTC, not just in the regulation of advertising, tended to proceed against small firms. The actual output from the FTC in formal complaints and 'cease and desist' orders in the 1960s is shown in Table 3.

The effect of this output on the actual tone of advertising and the behaviour of advertisers was not marked for a variety of reasons. The 'cease and desist' order was specific to a particular abuse and in practice there could be alternative equally deceptive claims made for the same product. Thus, repetitive offences by the same advertiser were not prevented. However, where a rare violation of an order was demonstrated, fines *per diem* were ordered. However, as Pitofsky,[29] a former Chairman of the FTC remarks:

Table 3. Number of FTC complaints and orders concerning false and misleading advertising

FTC output	1963	1964	1965	1966	1967	1968	1969
Complaints	127	129	66	48	108	45	65
Cease & desist orders	118	161	67	51	96	53	68

Source: American Bar Association, 'Report of the ABA Commission to Study the Federal Trade Commission', Chicago, 1969, p. 20.

'Since most advertising campaign themes run for a year or less, and most Commission advertising enforcement proceedings span periods of two to five years . . . the effect of any order was usually to direct the advertiser to discontinue an advertising campaign that had long since disappeared'.

Thus the various features: low chance of detection, the delay in proceeding, the requirement only to stop a particular advertisement all coalesce into a nugatory means of dealing with blatant advertising abuse. Indeed, the main beneficial effect of such a policy and sanctions is indirect, through the dissemination of an implicit standard of advertising practice, but of course this commends itself most to those who already are aware and commercially motivated to abide by their responsibilities. Although orders against such companies as Aluminium Company of America, General Motors, and the Ford Motor Company had been entered, the more blatant and deliberate frauds of small fly-by-night operators could persist unaffected by the general climate of what constituted acceptable advertising or the sanctions available in cases of its contravention.

A number of factors combined in the late 1960s and early 1970s to change the administration of advertising control. The activities of Ralph Nader and Edward Schwartz,[30] the moves against cigarette promotions, the organisation of the consumerist movement in general, and the critical reports of the FTC's performance in the American Bar Association Commission's report, in conjunction with the judgement in the Sperry and Hutchinson case (where the Supreme Court invited the FTC to consider 'public values beyond simply those enshrined in the letter or encompassed in the spirit of anti-trust laws'[31]), brought both a new determination and a consumer focus to bear. The 1975 Magnuson-Moss Act extended and clarified the FTC's powers. The issue of unfairness in advertising was interpreted to extend the right to advertise, by the issue of a trade regulation rule to pre-empt State laws which imposed certain restrictions on the advertising of eye glasses and eye examinations.[32] But this was subsequently suspended by a court of appeal which questioned whether the FTC had exceeded its authority. Subsequently, the Federal Trade Commission's Improvement Act 1980 imposed certain requirements on the FTC's rule-making activities and subjected them to Congressional Veto. The effect has been to limit the FTC's use of unfairness as justification for trade regulation rules concerning advertising, but its activities towards deception are not curtailed.[33]

By the 1975 Act, the FTC may proceed from one litigated case to require an entire class of unfair or deceptive advertisements to cease, subject to civil penalties if the FTC sues for violation of its rules. Moreover, to take the incentive out of unfairness and deception, there are provisions for the rescision or reformation of contracts, refund of money or return of property, payment of compensatory damages, and public notification. Advertisers must also meet FTC demands for the substantiation of their claims, to make affirmative disclosures of product information, and may be required to provide corrective advertising. Further detail and description of these provisions and the meanings and interpretations given to the terms 'unfair' and 'deceptive' in an advertising context follow.

The FTC's power rests on the interpretation of the terms 'unfair' and 'deceptive' and stems directly from the original 1914 Act which the various investigations, amendments and extensions since have done little to affect. It is significant that in 1914 Congress noted 'it is impossible to frame definitions which embrace all unfair practices'.[34] Indeed, the definitional questions that arise are crucial to the effectiveness of the FTC in achieving its objectives. Yet by its very nature, advertising is likely to contravene some standard of deceptiveness unless all possibilities for ambiguity, qualification and exaggeration are eradicated and only total truthfulness remains. Indeed, there is evidence that the remedial statements to correct misleading and deceptive advertisements, themselves can be misleading.[35] But the standard which the FTC must employ is in an environment where advertising is not characterised by literal truthfulness and so an intelligible but still arbitrary standard must be defined, and this standard must be one which permits the identification of a violation and provides the basis for prosecution. Thus, whilst as a literary exercise virtually any advertisement could be shown to have the capacity to deceive someone, in practice the extent of deception and the notion of some kind of representative advertising recipient or consumer is also necessary; moreover, this standard must be adapted as cultural and legal circumstances warrant.

The Commissioners of the FTC and the administrative law judge before whom initial hearings are held, can rely on their own intuitive understanding of the nature and extent of deception in an advertisement or consult more widely. In 3337 cases classed as deception by the FTC up until 1973, some 87 per cent were supported by internal evidence alone[36] (not all these cases involved advertising exclusively). The categories of external evidence, by contrast, were the use of dictionary definitions, trade definitions, expert testimony, and evidence from consumers and other sources. The use of external sources as reinforcement for the Commissioners' views, however, has shown a tendency to increase as the need for objective standards has been more keenly appreciated. Also, to the extent that the more conspicuous types of advertising abuse are no longer employed, the identification and pursuit of more subtle deceits require wider substantiation, including the surveying of consumers — a tactic also employed by the defence in contested cases. But external evidence is itself not incontrovertible or definitive. Thus Cohen[37] comments:

'At the present time it appears that the science of measuring consumer perception is imprecise. The grant of authority to the commission to determine meaning may be due to the administrative inconvenience of alternative approaches.'

Nevertheless, the case for greater use of external evidence has been urged by Rotfeld and Preston,[38] especially since Preston[39] has consistently argued that *puffery* — descriptions that cannot be objectively disproved — carries implications that deceive a substantial proportion of recipients. Moreover, to the extent that advertisers are required to substantiate objective claims, they might be inclined to make more nebulous, even vacuous, claims and thereby avoid the substantiation requirement. In the case where puffs nevertheless lead some consumers to perceive these as facts, they have a capacity to deceive and therefore should not be excluded from regulation merely because the FTC interprets puffs not as a statement of fact but of opinion.

It must still be determined which kind of person is likely to be deceived by advertising claims in general or puffs in particular and, furthermore, the objective standard of deception. Because such definitions are inherently concerned with the levels of knowledge and the intelligence and intellectual abilities of people, the ramifications of any definitions are immense. If the chosen standard is of the reasonable, uninformed person, then many more messages would be unexceptionable than under a definition that assumed naivety, stupidity and gullibility. The standard has indeed changed through time: from the 1920s' view of the person who exercised the care and diligence of a reasonably prudent man with deception arising only for the most credulous and the very stupid, to a regard in the late 1930s that the law must protect the 'trusting as well as the suspicious' which subsequently could embrace also 'the ignorant, the unthinking and the credulous'. This latter standard, also referred to as 'the least reasonable man' principle, is distinguished from the reasonable man who *inter alia* is responsible for his own actions and is generally presumed to be unable to plead innocence from other laws on the basis of innate poor judgement or ignorance of the law.[40] In fact, the FTC has not always used this 'least reasonable man' standard and has recognised that unreasonable misunderstandings by the foolish and feebleminded should be precluded, though it should be retained for special audiences whose members are deemed vulnerable, e.g. children, the elderly, the handicapped, the ghetto dweller.[41]

Also inconsistent with the *capabilities* of the least reasonable man was the proposal that all advertisers' claims concerning the safety, performance, efficacy, characteristics or comparative price of any product or service should have the supporting documentation available for public inspection, because the least reasonable man is the least likely to avail himself of the opportunity. This proposal, in 1971, for a Truth in Advertising Act was not proceeded with but the FTC's advertising substantiation provisions do require that an advertiser substantiate his claims at its request and to their satisfaction. Indeed, following the Pfizer case in 1972 the advertiser must have 'a reasonable basis' for making a claim but it falls to the FTC to prove that a questioned claim appeared in advertising and that the company did not have sufficient basis before disseminating the claim. The responsibility in such cases is not confined to the advertiser himself but can extend to the advertising agency, a retailer who displays the advertisements or a celebrity who endorses the claim. Moreover, a reasonable basis for the claim is necessary even if it is true and the product performs as advertised, because otherwise a competitor would be unfairly deprived of the opportunity to have made sales.

The criteria for substantiation obviously depend upon the nature of the claim and the characteristics of the product, but the FTC can require all reports of testing, experiments, surveys and general data to be submitted. Such documentation might support an objective claim, but consumers' perception of the claims is also relevant as indeed is the Commission's determination of 'what consumers would do in their purchase decisions if they knew the truth about the product'.[42] To overcome the problem of dealing with trivial cases the FTC can evaluate the 'scale of the deception' and its 'materiality', weigh its effects on vulnerable groups or more generally on the public interest and then evaluate whether the market would provide corrective forces tending to nullify any deception or unfairness. In this regard the classification of the characteristics of goods is relevant. Some qualities are readily apparent both to consumers and producers and attempts to deceive about such qualities could be expected to be short-lived. More durable are the experience qualities of goods which only emerge after purchase and use, whilst credence qualities must be taken on trust. It is the experience and credence qualities that provide the greatest scope for deception and accordingly claims about safety, dependability, reliability and efficacy are ones which require the more comprehensive documentation. Exaggerated statements of opinion (puffs) do not require substantiation.

Where there is judged to be insufficient substantiation, the FTC may obtain the consent of the advertiser to withdraw the advertisement or amend it, to affirm some information previously omitted and to provide restitution in the form of full refunds for the products with inadequately substantiated claims. In certain product categories — drugs, food, cosmetics and medical devices — an injunction may temporarily prohibit certain claims. The 'cease and desist' order can also be coupled with an order for withdrawal of advertising for a product for a specified period of time unless the misleading impression given by previous false advertising is corrected. Such corrective advertising may also be required in the case of consent decrees — the only method available prior to 1975. The corrective advertising can be a proportion of planned media expenses for a future period or be related to past advertising expenses. The first consent decree order was directed at the ITT Continental Baking Co., marketers of Profile Bread. The advertised claim, that the bread was of weight reducing value because it had fewer calories per slice than ordinary bread, was challenged by the FTC as this claim only arose because Profile was more thinly sliced. The uncontested order meant that ITT had to cease and desist all advertisements for Profile Bread unless 25 per cent of media costs for subsequent advertising stated that it was not effective for weight reduction.

Sales of Profile Bread subsequently fell by one quarter. In another case, the significant economic penalty implied by a corrective advertising order is again demonstrated. Warner Lambert were served a 'cease and desist' order to correct claims that Listerine would prevent or lessen the severity of cold and sore throat symptoms. Ultimately, the Supreme Court refused to review the Court of Appeal's judgement and the company was required to publish corrective advertising until it had spent a sum equal to its average annual appropriation on this product for the previous ten years—about $10 m. In a further example, an initial decision by an Administrative Law judge ruled that American Home Products spend $24 m. on future advertising containing the statement 'Anacin is not a tension reliever' because there was inadequate scientific evidence to support their previously advertised claim.[43]

There are difficulties in enforcing corrective advertising, however. The FTC is obliged to avoid punitive action and must find justification to prove that the advertiser's false claim was believed, that it affected consumers' purchasing decisions and that the false belief could persist after the claim was stopped. From such difficulties and the response of advertisers to this measure the initial spate of correction orders has dramatically diminished.

1.5 Conclusions

In principle, policy measures directed at false, deceptive and misleading advertising and offending advertisers find widespread support both amongst consumers and responsible advertisers. It is in the formulation and implementation of practicable policy, however, that difficulties and anomalies occur and where criticisms of advertising regulatory practice arise. It is not particularly difficult to specify the sort of features which an *ideal* system should exhibit, for instance:

1. Advertising abuse should be unambiguously defined and universally recognisable.
2. Any abuse should be preventable prior to transmission.
3. The costs of prevention should rest exclusively with the advertiser.
4. Any adverse effects from errors of commission or omission should be fully compensated.
5. There should be no incentive to abuse the freedom to advertise.
6. Penalties should be swift, sure and/or conspicuous to deter possible offenders.

However, the problems of definition, identification, administration and execution are formidable and even with the best intentions the complexity and flexibility of advertising can always allow scope for abuse whether this be intended or involuntary. Arising, however, from advertising's conspicuousness is an inbuilt tendency for responsible advertisers to be in conformity with all recognised standards. Problems arise from differing perceptions of these standards and of degrees of compliance with them. However, such problems, when they become manifest, tend to be corrected because the responsible advertiser has the incentive to achieve improvement. It is also in his interest to *avoid* any notoriety that substantial criticism of his advertising would entail. Despite this, on occasions some contravention of the accepted standards can occur for a variety of reasons and, in the time it takes for withdrawal and amendment, adverse effects arise. More intractable is the problem of the unscrupulous free riding on the good reputation of advertisers in general: thus the fly-by-night advertiser abuses advertising and acquires private benefits (but imposes conspicuous costs on everyone else). This deliberate action clearly lacks any tendency to self-correction so methods to eradicate this abuse have to be found elsewhere. Again, the problem arises that the damage is already done when such advertising is withdrawn and the prevention of such abuse is clearly preferable. The necessary incentive and the power to deny such advertising space or time lie with the media, but their action depends on the identification of any abuse. In the case of a persistent offender employing successive media, the obligation to deny facilities becomes conspicuous. Less tractable is the identification of a potential advertising abuser. Here it is necessary to distinguish between those who use advertising in a proper fashion but whose subsequent or intended behaviour is injurious, and the abuser of advertising itself irrespective of intention or behaviour. In the latter case, effective scrutiny of advertisements prior to transmission should be possible and cumulating experience of the characteristics of general abusive advertising does reduce the scope, if not the incentive, for such advertising, but prior scrutiny of advertisements alone is largely ineffectual to prevent the former, except in the case of the habitual offender. Innocuous advertising itself holds no clues to its users' intentions.

It is unrealistic to presume that the individual and various perceptions of millions of recipients of millions of advertisements would not inevitably generate some complaints and, on occasions, demonstrable adverse effects. The intended obtrusiveness of advertising makes it particularly vulnerable to such charges whether these be legitimate, merely well-intentioned, malicious or frivolous. The problem is to determine the reliability of any complaint in a way proportionate to the scale of the 'offence'. In the UK the law has been seen and found inappropriate for this purpose because its institutional characteristics and rigidities make it frequently unsuitable for use by individuals aggrieved with, or adversely affected by, particular advertisements. The necessary precision of legal drafting and consequent questions of interpretation render the law continuously outdated and essentially impotent against the inherent flexibility of advertising in such cases where there is a deliberate intent to flout the law. Sufficiently large penalties would serve as a deterrent to significant abuse if these had an eventual chance of being exacted, but the character of such abuse is often trivial and such penalty disproportionate in comparison with the penalties for other offences. In a civil case, the court has greater discretion both in the assessment of damages and the award of costs: but the possible delay in bringing a case, the uncertainty of the outcome and the consequent likelihood of considerable, even exhorbitant, expense acts as a deterrent to its general use. Moreover, the legal process, when utilised by one advertiser against another, can provide not only a welcome and necessary means of protection and redress but also a way of gaining publicity or imposing delay and/or costs.

Given the general efficacy of advertising and the benign characteristics of the vast majority of advertisements it is unsurprising that advertiser self-regulation should have evolved. The industry absorbs the costs of regulation, itself has the means to prevent transmission, and has a vested interest in obviating both abuse and its concomitant criticism. However, it too faces the problem of anticipating the incidence of any offence, a balance in cost, time and power in the vetting of advertisements, preventing abuse and policing standards. How adequate its incentives are, and whether the extent and efficiency of self regulation are judged to be sufficient, is a matter for detailed and expert assessment.

The impartial scrutineers of the self-regulatory system have generally found it to be both effective and responsive, and the industry's self-interest in achieving acceptable and improved advertising offers greater scope than the alternatives in the prevention of significant abuse of advertising. The non-legalistic formulation of codified standards and the flexibility of inter-pretations, and the power to both initiate improvements and respond as occasion requires are all in keeping with the characteristics of advertising and appropriate to the only marginal adjustments that might be required. Such a system, however, is not likely to consider the efficacy of advertising as an institution or the more quantitative aspects associated with the volume of advertisements, nor, indeed, to consider its wider effects, which are the subject of the next chapter.

References

1. Lindblom, C. E., 'The Science of Muddling Through', *Public Administration Review*, 1958.
2. Advertising Standards Authority, *Code of Advertising Practice*, London, 6th edition, 1979.
3. Smith, P. and Swann, D., *Protecting the Consumer*, Oxford: Martin Robertson & Co., 1979, p.144.
4. Cornish, W. R., *Intellectual Property: Patents, Copyright, Trademarks and Allied Rights*, London: Sweet & Maxwell, 1981, p.9, p.11.

5. *Ibid.*, pp.505–7.
6. Smith and Swann, *op.cit.*, pp.23–5.
7. Boddewyn, J. J., 'Outside Participation in Advertising Self Regulation: The Case of the Advertising Standards Authority (U.K.)', *Journal of Consumer Policy*, Vol. 6, No. 1, 1983, pp.77–93..
8. Office of Fair Trading, *Review of the UK Self-regulatory system of advertising Control*, Nov. 1978, p.27.
9. *Ibid.*
10. *Ibid.*, p.36, para. 4.41.
11. *Ibid.*, p.33.
12. *Ibid.*, p.34, para. 4.33.
13. *Ibid.*, p.35.
14. *Ibid.*, p. (1), para. 3.
15. *Ibid.*, p.44.
16. *Official Journal of the European Communities*, No. C 70/4, 21.3.78.
17. Department of Trade, *The Self Regulatory System of Advertising Control—Report of Working Party*, London, 1980, p.2.
18. *Ibid.*, p.2.
19. House of Lords Select Committee on the European Communities, 'Misleading Advertising', *38th Report*, 1977–78.
20. *Ibid.*, p.X (iv).
21. House of Commons, Select Committee on European Legislation, 'Misleading and Unfair Advertising', *33rd Report*, 1977–78, p.4.
22. *Official Journal of the European Communities*, No. C 194/3, 1.8.79.
23. House of Lords Select Committee on the European Communities' 'Misleading Advertising', *26th Report*, 1979–80.
24. Department of Trade, *op. cit.* p. 8, para. 16.
25. Department of Trade, *ibid.*, p.8.
26. House Report 1613, 75th Congress, 1st Session, 4 1937. Quoted by Cohen, D., ' "The Unfairness Doctrine" and Consumer Advertising', in Ferrell, O. C. and LaGarce, R. (eds.), *Public Policy Issues in Marketing*, Lexington, Mass.: Lexington Books, 1975, pp.67–72.
27. Bogart, L., *Strategy in Advertising*, New York: Harcourt, Brace & World, 1967, p.2. Quoted by Stone, A., *Economic Regulation and the Public Interest: The Federal Trade Commission in Theory and Practice*, Ithaca and London: Cornell University Press, 1977, p.66.
28. Posner, R., *Economic Analysis of Law*, Boston, Mass.: Little Brown & Co., 1972, pp.389–90.
29. Pitofsky, R., 'Advertising Regulation and the Consumer Movement', in Therck, D. G. (ed.), *Issues in Advertising: The Economics of Persuasion*, Washington, D.C.: American Enterprise Institute for Public Policy Research, 1978, p.42.
30. Udell, G. C. and Fischer, P. J., 'The FTC Improvement Act', *Journal of Marketing*, vol. 41, no. 2, 1977, pp.81–6. These authors cite FTC v. Sperry and Hutchinson Co., 405 US 233 (1972). See also 'Legal Developments in Marketing', *Journal of Marketing*, vol. 36, no. 4, 1972, p.64.

31. Stone, *Economic Regulation and the Public Interest*, p.206, and FTC v. Sperry and Hutchinson Co., 92 S.Ct. 898, 905 (1972).
32. FTC Trade Regulation Rules, Advertising of Ophthalmic Goods and Services, 1978.
33. Cohen, D., 'Unfairness in Advertising Revisited', *Journal of Marketing*, vol. 46, Winter 1982, pp.73–80, p.75.
34. *House Report*, No. 1142, 63rd Congress, 2nd Session, 18, 1914.
35. Jacoby, J., Nelson, M. C. and Hoyer, W. D., 'Corrective Advertising and Affirmative Disclosure Statements: Their Potential for confusing and misleading the Consumer', *Journal of Marketing*, vol. 46, Winter 1982, pp.61–72.
36. Brandt, M. T. and Preston, I. L. 'The Federal Trade Commission's Use of Evidence to Determine Deception', *Journal of Marketing*, Vol. 44, No. 1, 1977, pp. 54–62.
37. Cohen, D., 'The FTC's Advertising Substantiation Program', *Journal of Marketing*, vol. 44, no. 1, 1980, p.30.
38. Rotfeld, H. J. and Preston, I. L., 'The Potential Impact of Research on Advertising Law', *Journal of Advertising Research*, vol. 21, no. 2, 1981, pp.9–17.
39. Preston, I. L., *The Great American Blow-Up: Puffery in Advertising and Selling*, Madison: University of Wisconsin Press, 1975; 'The FTC's Handling of Puffery and Other Selling Claims Made "By Implication"', *Journal of Business Research*, vol. 5, 1977, pp.155–81.
40. Cunningham, I. C. M., and Cunningham, W. H., 'Standards for Advertising Regulation', *Journal of Marketing*, vol. 41, no. 4, 1977, pp.92–7.
41. Cohen, 'The "Unfairness Doctrine" and Consumer Advertising', p.69.
42. FTC, DNA and OPPE, *FTC Policy Planning Protocol for Substantiation Actions*, quoted by Cohen, D., 'The FTC's Advertising Substantiation Program', p.28.
43. *Trade Regulation Reporter*, 'In re American Home Products Corp. et al', 3 (September) No. 21, 380.

2

Economics and advertising policy

2.1 Introduction

Chapter 1 considers aspects of advertising regulation in a largely non-disciplinary framework, with emphasis given to the control of particular abuses within a context of generally acceptable advertising. In discussing the disciplinary view of economics and its relation to advertising policy in this chapter and the next, it is necessary to consider the basis of an economic approach, the modes of analysis employed to the generality of advertising, and the scope and means of any regulation, including the standing of the economist in this respect.

The essence of an economic approach to advertising is in terms of the costs and benefits of advertisements. The placing of an advertisement is a commercial transaction with paid media, agency and production expenses of various kinds; but the transaction concept can be extended to include the outlay not only of money but also of effort and time, with benefits in turn being both pecuniary and non-pecuniary. Benefits and costs accordingly can be experienced both by those directly involved in advertising — the advertiser and his target audience/recipients — but also, more widely, by other producers and casual recipients, for instance. In this terminology, regulation, in principle, seeks to increase the benefits and/or reduce the costs so that net returns, inclusive of the resource cost of regulation itself, are increased. The pathological concerns of the previous chapter — false, misleading and deceptive advertising — can be viewed as imposing costs on consumers and other producers with benefits accruing only, or mainly, to the perpetrators. Overall, the issue of the regulation of advertising involves determination of the general benefits net of costs of advertising, with the pathological cases serving to increase the costs, but with due concern also being accorded to distribution of both benefits and costs.

Such a comprehensive evaluation has not been conducted and almost certainly could not be conducted but on other bases, arguments and evidence, economics has influenced the conception and implementation of regulatory policy and has broadened the scope for regulation beyond the context of false and misleading advertising. The nature and consequences of such an influence, like most matters concerning advertising policy, is an area of considerable controversy involving the justification, the extent and the means of any regulation; a controversy which rages amongst economists but also more generally, as bluntly stated by Cohen[1] when from a psychologist's perspective he cautions:

'so long as we have economists in our midst we shall need to be alert to the trick of letting value judgements masquerade as statements of fact'.

In considering the relationship between economics, economists and policy, it is useful to distinguish three resultant main bodies of opinion from the many shades that abound. First, there are those who view economics as scientific endeavour where the scientist can be detached from any policy issue *qua* scientist: thus economics may be pursued in the neutral or positive fashion with any normative implications clearly separate from positive analysis. Policy options can be positively analysed, but any choice between options and the selection of criteria on which to base judgement move the economist from the positive domain, a step which is clearly recognisable. Secondly, economics can be employed to designate the ordering of concepts, methods and results to further policy predilections: the economist becomes the advocate of some explicit objective which may be predominantly economic in character but need not necessarily be so. Those in this category differ in the extent of the frankness of their exposition on policy objectives; some are overtly propagandist, others pursue their objectives by more subtle means. The third group is less precisely defined; its members recognise that sufficient detachment to remove totally predilection or sympathy or orientation from an analytical/scientific enquiry is impossible. The possibility that analysis is implicitly oriented to policy objectives cannot be ignored (although its influence may be small, nevertheless) and this recognition necessitates the widest appraisal of both analysis and prescription.[2]

In terms of this categorisation, it is only the first group — broadly, the logical positivists — who conceive that their analyses are neutral with respect to policy issues. That is, their selection of assumptions, the nature of their abstractions, the choice of analytical technique and the interpretation of deductions are, they claim, entirely free of value judgement and predilection. It is therefore possible to define policy options analytically within this framework and to relegate the choice of options to a subsequent and separate process. This approach is not confined to theoretical work alone. Its extension to empirical work is both possible and extensively practised. Empirical tests, within conventional methodology, are themselves viewed as neutral. That is, the attenuated process of conceiving of a model, selecting data and evaluating results are all value-free activities whose relevance to policy is independent of the orientations of the researcher and whose results are free of a selective bias.[3]

Adjudication on the merits of the various methodological and policy positions outlined above transcends economic considerations and depends on philosophical dispositions which in turn are beyond resolution. At best, all that can be achieved is to demonstrate the nature of the problem as it relates to advertising.

If it is proposed to extend regulation beyond the control of misleading and false advertising, then the question of whether regulation *per se* is efficacious does not necessarily arise; after all, the control of misleading and false advertising evolved to meet a conspicuous need and it might at first sight seem reasonable that any extension of regulation could be so justified on evolutionary grounds. But where the proposed extension is in a qualitatively different direction, this does not apply and the case for it must be made. That pressure for regulation does not arise from economic theory is apparent from Needham:[4]

'Whilst public policy towards pricing behaviour is based, at least in part, upon conclusions derived from economic theory, the same cannot be said of policy towards advertising. Economic theory provides no clear policy guidelines in the case of advertising. Few people would deny that a clear case can be made for laws to protect consumers against false or misleading advertising; what, however, can be said regarding evils of advertising which do not fall into this category?'.

Also, in a more restricted context Comanor and Wilson[5] are unable to find theoretical justification:

'We find that the theoretical studies of advertising and competition are not compelling and that our conclusions must rest on the empirical results.'

But once the empirical evidence is assessed, in terms that clearly reveal the degree of controversy surrounding the extension of regulation, they conclude:

'The weight of available evidence is consistent with the hypothesis that heavy advertising can have substantial anti-competitive consequences . . . no policy implications of this result follow directly . . . In large measure, the current controversy regarding advertising applies more to the policy implications of this finding than the finding itself.'[6]

It must be noted that the debate is further complicated by the fact that they are accused by Block[7] of 'selective acceptance of the available evidence'.

It will be necessary to consider some of these aspects in greater detail, but initially we consider the societal context for any extension of advertising regulations in terms of the concept of negative freedoms.

2.2 Negative freedoms

Advertising is a form of social communication and a society which values the right of free expression could not maintain the value of this general right and simultaneously deny the right to advertise. But the freedom of expression is itself not unqualified nor unlimited and to include advertising with this right is to presume certain limitations on it, too. The concept of negative freedom refers to the right to exercise a right, providing it does not infringe the negative freedoms of others to exercise their rights. The number and extent of negative freedoms are such that the interactions in society lead to negative freedoms impinging on each other, both in the individual and between individuals. Although some negative freedoms are complementary others conflict, so the scope for the simple aggregation of freedoms is thereby circumscribed. But such is the interaction of society that some resolution must be found and it is the formal institutional arrangements and the mores of a culture which define the nature and scope of particular freedoms, and which order freedoms in appropriate rankings dependent on circumstances. Clearly then, freedom of expression may be subordinate to superior rights; thus there may be coercion through the state, which exercises the right of subpoena or freedom of expression may be curtailed in the interests of secrecy. In general the law may be regarded as a formalisation of the ranking of rights in a variety of circumstances but the order that arises from the mores of a culture may be as effective, or indeed more effective than the law in establishing precedents, though the power which is exercised is differently based. Some form of power is essential for the maintenance of negative freedoms but superior power — either constitutionally legitimate or more informally based — enables the pursuit of positive aims which may be inimical to negative freedoms.

If the right to advertise is considered a negative freedom, as part of the wider freedom of expression, then many of the institutional restrictions on this freedom in general apply equally to advertising — thus libel, slander, incitement, profanity, obscenity, etc. are circumscribed by law. Despite the fact that it is impossible to find communication aspects of advertising which do not have their counterparts in other forms of expression, advertising may be considered to warrant more attention outside the context of free expression where other negative freedoms are violated either directly, for example, due to advertising's intrusiveness or indirectly due to its possible power to influence action.

By the fundamental characteristic of advertising — that it is impersonal communication through paid media (which distinguishes it from a wide variety of other signs and ways of communicating) — it is clear that other negative freedoms are indeed involved. An economic freedom to trade in space and time is a negative freedom, separate from the right to communicate that is due to both advertiser and media owners. The right to trade is as fundamental as the right to free expression but it too is institutionally circumscribed by the exercise of power or influence enforcing superior rights. Thus certain types of trade are typically either illegal or morally reprehensible; for instance, trade in slaves, corpses, prostitutes, pornography, stolen goods and drugs affronts accepted standards and in advertising such goods the media owner would incur similar disfavour, if not a legal penalty, precisely because society sees these as 'bads' rather than goods. Even if this is not formalised in law, the media owner may exercise discretion in trade and deny advertising facilities, perhaps to ensure the continued patronage of other advertisers and thereby a practical boundary of the joint freedoms of trade and expression is defined. Where the advertising of such products and services is itself not illegal, such communication about illicit products would be restricted to specialised media or perhaps be disseminated by transparent codes as euphemisms or slang. If the demand is sufficient, so that both suppliers and consumers have an unfulfilled need, illicit media may even appear. In effect, a sub-culture of freedom of expression and trade emerges.

Logically related to the legal advertising of an illicit product, is the illegal advertising of a legitimate product. Many examples are apparent, depending on the precise meaning given to the term 'legal' advertising — the UK ban on the television advertising of cigarettes and the ban on advertising by certain professional groups provide examples. The enforced separation of the rights to communicate and to trade is a curtailment of negative freedoms for a superior objective, but not necessarily one selected with a due regard for the preservation of negative freedoms.

Examples of the partial limitation on the freedoms to communicate and to trade are the cases of the restrictions on the amount and distribution of advertising on UK television and (in contrast to the US) the requirement that advertising and programme content have no explicit connection. The desired objective is the avoidance of commercial pressure to the detriment of a public service. Similarly, there is fear that the advertising 'subsidy' to (particularly national) newspapers could compromise editorial freedoms; in this case the trade — rather than the communication — aspect of advertising is in potential conflict with another form of the freedom of expression. However, the recent growth of 'free sheets' is an example of advertising, not only itself communicating, but by total subsidisation providing new scope for editorial expression.

This brief discussion of the relationship between the freedoms of expression and trade demonstrates that choices must be made between negative freedoms. Indeed, following Machlup[8], further negative freedoms including moral, intellectual and political freedoms must also be taken into account.

If our earlier consideration of advertising policy is appraised against this conceptual background of negative freedoms, the general presumption that there is effectively a right to advertise clearly emerges. So too does the moral (and often legally enforceable) obligation that advertising should not impinge upon the freedoms of competitors, recipients and consumers. Thus, the concern with fairness and the proscription of deceit are as appropriate in an advertising context as in other areas of human activity. But, although there is a consensus on these matters, there are considerable conflicts of interest, opinion and, indeed, ideology. At the most fundamental level there are difficulties in the rankings and priorities of constituent negative freedoms, whilst in marginal areas, the problems of definition and administration can be no less intractable for those involved. But, although the evolution of advertising has included some measures to regulate abuse to meet both producer and consumer interests, the principles of and criteria for advertiser accountability are increasingly to the fore, at least in the UK, EEC and USA contexts. The issue is not whether there should be some regulation — for this is generally accepted — but what form this regulatory mechanism should take, how its powers should be determined, who is to administer them, how responsive, objective and accountable is the mechanism to be to the perceived problems of advertising abuse, how is abuse to be detected and what will be the economic implications?

Even from the premise that the overwhelming majority of advertisements routinely avoid contravening society's accepted standards, whether these are formal or informal, radically opposed approaches to advertising regulation are apparent which differ with respect to the implications for negative freedoms. On the one hand, the onus can be placed on the advertiser to show either no fault or full compliance with accepted standards, and on the other, the advertiser should be accountable when fault is demonstrated. Both these proposals are consistent with the preservation of negative freedom: the advertiser should not impinge on the freedoms of others and, where he does, some form of retribution is appropriate, but nor should the advertiser's rights to expression be compromised unduly nor an economic penalty effectively be imposed in gaining compliance. If the initial fault and the means of retribution are predominantly economic in character, the costs of regulation and the costs imposed on all parties must also be considered, as must the offsetting benefits — an economic task which economics is not, in fact, equipped to undertake.

The combination of the lack of a comprehensive, theoretical and empirical appraisal of advertising, of the predispositions and orientations of individual economists, and of the inevitable departure from purely disciplinary confines involved in the advocacy of economic policy, is sufficient to ensure that there is a considerable range of policy measures suggested in the relevant literature, none of which enjoys universal acceptance. But the extent of analytical economic enquiry, of both theoretical and empirical kinds, is disproportionately meagre as justification for the policy recommendations that have been put forward. Some indication of this is provided by the recent survey of the economics of advertising undertaken by Chiplin and Sturgess.[9] Towards the end of their book, these authors correctly conclude that the policy implications of their preceding analysis are slight:

'Our discussions have indicated that there is no consensus in economics concerning the net benefit or cost of advertising to society. Much here depends on the value judgements of the particular individual. There are, therefore, no clear-cut policy recommendations. In the remainder of this chapter we shall discuss the forms of policy towards advertising that have been suggested, while leaving the reader to decide whether any or all of the policies are necessary and if so, the precise way in which they should be implemented.'[10]

It is not our purpose to survey the economics of advertising in its many aspects: rather, our concern is with the influence of particular facets of economic analysis on policy. This more specific concern is based upon the belief that many conventional topics in the economics of advertising be so edited or combined that the essential policy issues, which would otherwise be buried in a welter of analytical detail, may stand out. Such an approach has obvious limitations, but the critical examination of public policy towards advertising *necessitates* an overview of this sort. The alternative is to conduct the discussion of advertising economics at such an elevated level of abstraction or at such a level of detail that concrete policy issues and implications become lost in the process of intellectual refinement. Even in distinguishing the salient topics of 'advertising and information' and 'advertising and competition', we may be introducing an unreal distinction since competition (and collusion) depends vitally upon information (although Albion and Farris do draw a strict dichotomy[11]). Nevertheless, the selection of 'advertising and competition' for discussion permits the subsumation of such considerations as advertising and price, product differentiation, concentration and barriers to entry, as well as so many other topics conventionally analysed primarily within the structure–conduct–performance paradigm.[12] Our aim after all is not to rehearse in typical textbook fashion those parts of economic analysis which can be squeezed into a discussion of advertising, but to demonstrate the need for a more thorough investigation of consumers' and producers' behaviours (see Chapters 4 and 5) and of economic relationships (Chapter 3) than is usually possible within the conventional — neoclassical — framework. Our selection of these topics is further justified by the observation that the major policy recommendations which stem from economic analysis have been based primarily upon a rationale conceived in terms of competition and information.

2.3 Advertising and information

The advertiser employs advertising to transmit a message which is intended to benefit him and which is selected by a deliberate process, involving consideration of alternative means of communicating with consumers. An advertisement identifies the advertiser and his product or service. In a culture which is familiar with advertisements, the explicit partiality of advertising as a means of communication is recognised and is itself unremarkable. It is, after all, almost impossible to conceive of any form of communication which is not partial in one sense or another. Advertising, however, is criticised for some or all of the following reasons: it is repetitive, frequent, insistent, subtle, insidious, overwhelming, ubiquitous, and generally, it is thought, cumulates into a form of communication which has some specific power over our action; to both change and initiate action. This action, whilst it may benefit the advertising recipient, is primarily to the benefit of the advertiser himself. To counterbalance the power which the command of advertising resources can bestow, Kaldor,[13] Meade[14] and Reekie[15] have argued that alternative independent information should be made available.

There is an underlying presumption that information is an indispensable input to decision-making and in the presence of incomplete or misleading information, less than totally efficacious decisions will be made. Thus there may be a role for action in the centralised provision of information. Meade[16] claims, for example, that:

'It is desirable for the state to discourage private commercial advertisement and to foster disinterested consumer research and information services',

while Kaldor[17] expresses the view that such services would be inexpensive:

'Thus the cost of an independent information service about commodities — quite disregarding the great improvements in the quality and the quantity of information which it would bring about — could only amount to a fraction of the present cost of advertising to the community.'

The service provided by independent information sources such as consumers organisations and the compilers of guides, gazetteers and lists of all kinds are viewed as a model for the kind of information provision that a more co-ordinated and extensive system would impart. The gross figures of advertising expenditure are noted and it is deduced that an extremely adequate, if not luxurious, independent information system could be run for sums of that magnitude. This is plausible but requires further consideration.

Advertising expenditure is the accumulation of independent outlays by myriad advertisers, some of whom, on the basis of judgement on their own criteria, justify large appropriations whilst others in similar circumstances spend less. To the recipient, advertising is a free good — he makes no explicit outlay for receipt of the advertisements themselves — though the recovery of advertising costs may be included in the product price along with all other expenditures incurred by producers. In contrast, the subscription to consumer organisations or the outright purchase of guides involves explicit outlay. In fact, utilisation currently made of such fee-charging independent information sources is miniscule compared with the potential, but the non-zero price of their services is a contributory, though not the prevailing, reason for the modest uptake of their facilities. Even if these information services were without price, their use would not be, one suspects, dramatically increased, for information processing involves time and effort and thus imposes a cost on the decision maker.

In general, the art of advertising is to transmit a message which is simple so that no great demand is made on the time or mental facilities of its recipients. The advertiser does not seek to provide comprehensive information but the information he provides may, nevertheless, be sufficient for the consumers' needs and advertised information may fulfil the function of obviating an elaborate and costly decision process, or of reducing this process to more manageable component parts. It is not that advertisers only provide simplistic advertised messages, they also may — especially for more complex and expensive items — provide extensive information on request, or in some supplementary form such as brochures, trained sales staff, etc. The initial advertisement may contribute to the entire process by signifying the possibility of a decision, thereby prompting further research, or by providing sufficient information to remove that suggestion from any further consideration. Even the availability of comprehensive information would require some means of easy access for similar 'termination' or 'proceed' decisions. The relative paucity of 'hard information' in advertisements (for instance, the study of US TV commercials by Resnik and Stern[18] found that only half contained hard information), suggests that the function of advertising is often intended by advertisers to be an alert to the possibility of a decision rather than the provision of the means to analyse and arrive at a decision. By the provision of *appropriate* information, the advertiser may achieve both the formulation of a decision and provide an acceptable solution to it, thereby reducing the costs of decision to a minimum.

Although information is in some sense indispensable to decision-making — at least to the extent that it directs a decision — the actual form and content of information is crucial if it is to contribute positively to a decision rather than unduly to complicate or even frustrate it. Also, on occasion, the advertising provides information pertaining to a decision which the recipient neither wants nor appreciates. The advertiser, however, cannot know precisely what is required, for recipients may not even know themselves. Moreover, individuals have different requirements which also change through time whether they receive advertising messages or not. The advertising system which provides information of a selected kind is clearly susceptible to criticism on innumerable counts. However, the argument that it *has* evolved, and is constantly adapting and evolving as new and old advertisers seek new messages for both existing and new audiences, and that it thereby seeks improvements in information provision must be judged against the alternatives.

The critics view the unregulated provision of information in advertisements as broadly excessive in amount, with failings in objectivity and content. For instance, in a US context, Congressman Rosenthal[19] has stated that:

'As technology advances, products become more sophisticated and there is a greater need to analyse a product before making a judgement about it. Yet, in buying drugs, for example, none of us can make any kind of efficacious judgement, even though the costs of advertising, merchandising and distributing pharmaceuticals is about seven to ten times the cost of research. That offends me.'

These observations prompt activity on two fronts: measures to restrict the amount of advertising in areas where it does not fulfil a useful information function, and either the requirement that advertisements should convey particular information or that such information should be forthcoming from alternative sources. In any event, the problems raised are considerable.

The provision and utilisation of information are not costless activities. Information which has a prior, recognised value may warrant consumers' direct payments, but the organisation of means of collection, the difficulty of conceptualising precisely what is the benefit, and the mainly small sums involved make the application of this principle difficult for the vast majority of advertisements. Because these are deliberately simplified, the information service they provide is thereby limited. Nevertheless, often the scale of advertising reaching many individuals ensures that the overall gain in information — a reduction of the transaction costs associated with product purchase — is likely to exceed the advertiser's outlay in communicating that information. Indeed this is the most compelling economic reason for the existence and continued use of advertising. (Note the similarity of this to the argument that the harm done to the individual through falsity may be miniscule but that its cumulative effect upon the aggregate of consumers justifies collective action; a regulatory power is instituted to prevent this harm.) In the absence of advertising this type of information would not be forthcoming and it remains to be established what would replace it and under what conditions. If the advertised information was *without* information value its replacement would not be necessary, but to ascertain what its value is, with the objective of replacing it in a more efficient manner is a task of daunting complexity. Doubtless for the reason that individual assessment is an impossible task, given the vast variety of circumstances and the infinite number of messages for myriad goods, the problem has been tackled more selectively. Thus an advertising ban presumes that advertising either makes an insufficient net positive contribution, or is actually harmful, for instance in encouraging purchase or use of what are deemed 'bads'. A ban on one form of communication, however, may lead to the increased use of alternatives, and to this extent the information argument unavoidably, in terms of economics at least, must deal with alternative means of promotion. These may take many forms including the use of sponsorship, competitions and sales force activity but it is a characteristic of economic discussion that advertising is merely illustrative of many forms of sales promotion which are associated with particularly oligopolistic market structures. The main thrust of the competition case against advertising (see below), would wish to reduce not only advertising but sales promotion expenditure as well. Short of an actual ban, certain themes may be identified as non-productive in terms of their likely information content and thus advertising can be subjected to some form of monitoring with abuses detected, penalties exacted and deficiencies rectified. To reduce the enforcement costs some form of agreement with advertisers to abstain from certain advertising practices, or to limit expenditure or restrict advertising to specialist audiences may be possible for specific products. The prevention of advertisements for contraceptives in general, or the ban on cigarette advertising on television are examples. This being impractical for all products, a means proposed is some form of tax on advertising to reduce the gross amount. As Meade[20] argues:

'A tax on advertisement would increase the incentive for firms to seek markets by cutting prices rather than by persuasive bamboozlement . . .'

Each of these methods seeks to avoid or curtail the detrimental aspects identified in particular advertisements or in advertising in general; our premise earlier was to envisage an information system which at least provided the *benefits* of advertising in a cost-effective fashion. For the vast majority of goods there can be little doubt that sufficient benefits do accrue (to both advertisers and recipients) so that its use is maintained.

The argument that the evolution of the advertising system provides generally acceptable advertisements is countered by those who see the advertising industry as a gigantic evil to which individual (generally) well-intentioned businessmen collectively contribute to a system which is to the ultimate detriment of themselves and society. As will be seen (in Chapter 3 and reference 4), members of the Austrian school of economics (notably Hayek and Lackmann) consider the subject matter of economics to be about the *unintended* consequences of action but, of course, it must be established whether the system *is* 'acceptable' or 'evil', which raises questions about the nature of the evolutionary process that gives rise to the phenomenon. It is our understanding that this requires analysis of 'competition' which is discussed further in this chapter and in the next.

An alternative information transmission system depends on the solution of two main problems: the selection of the types of information that would be transmitted and finding the necessary finance. The two are not unrelated because if the content and amount met recipient demand at a price they were prepared to pay, then the service of information provision could be self-financing.

The problem of assembling and disseminating information packages in a form suitable for charge would be formidable. On the presumption that existing provision must be maintained or enhanced, the accumulation of bits of information into saleable clusters capable of sustaining wide distribution would encounter opposing difficulties. For the breadth of coverage, concise but comprehensive information is desirable, but this is unselective and certain audiences would benefit little from such generalised compilations. In the face of this, only a low cover charge would be feasible, but it is likely that the project would not be self-financing at such a level. This in turn raises the question which is probably at the heart of the issue: should privately-supplied advertising information — for its imperfections — be replaced by some form of public information service subject to total or partial subsidy?

The most comprehensive — and therefore most impracticable — means of such information provision would be the replacement of privately advertised and uncoordinated measures by a totally centralised information system where information would be available either free or at a nominal charge from the authorised source, which could determine the nature of the information and the conditions of its availability. The provision of centralised information is ultimately only consistent with a centralised system of economic admin- istration in general, because the lack of co-ordination associated with the separation of information provision and production eventually requires remedial action by the state. For instance, if finished goods lack informed purchasers, planned inventories suffer dislocation which affects both suppliers and distributors who are forced to modify their plans, which in turn influences the production, information and distribution plans of other products and so on throughout an economy. Dislocation on this scale is only amenable to a central solution, at least in principle, but it is instructive to note that countries with this system have a 'private' sector of advertising in any event, presumably because it is more responsive under decentralised control to perceive information needs, whether these are in producer or consumer sectors. In any event, this system shares the 'defect' of private advertising: that the recipient is effectively paying for advertising (through higher prices, or taxes, etc.), whether or not he values the information that is transmitted. The view that the private levying of a charge through higher prices for useless information is reprehensible, whilst the same effects from a public source are acceptable, is obviously not based on economic logic.

The 'public good' aspect of information (that all benefit if it is available and that separate charge is infeasible on those who specifically use it and, therefore, that some collective provision is appropriate), whilst true in principle, is of strictly limited application in practice. The compatibility of publicly-supplied information with private commercial incentives is unlikely. If the information system is backed by the resources of the state, there is scope for the ultimate direction of resources, tantamount to central planning and, prior to that, the impartiality of information is likely to be the subject of continuous litigation. To avoid such an embroilment the state as an alternative may encourage an independent service, perhaps financed by a grant or indeed a tax on existing advertising. The independent agency would be the purveyor of information judged appropriate to the major categories of demand — any hope of providing a comprehensive service is recognised (as indeed it must be) as impracticable. The tax on advertising is designed simultaneously to reduce the amount of advertising by effectively making its use more expensive, and the amount of partial information which independent information must counter. The

difficulty of identifying the appropriate categories of information is a fundamental limitation of this scheme. The presumption is that advertising is merely
factual and that fuller facts or the analysis of facts are sufficient to neutralise the
perceived effects of advertising. This is clearly not likely to be the case:
advertising is factual in the above sense only to a small degree, its appeals are
not only to rational objective assessment, but to a wide range of emotional and
subjective needs. The neutralisation of such appeals is not only impossible but
the attempt to do this would add a whole new dimension to the fears of
manipulation of thought and action.

   The co-existence of privately- or publicly-funded independent information
bureaux with advertising in its present or reduced form has little to commend
it. There is reason to suspect that its performance would not meet the requirements that its existence would need to generate, given that the demand for
information is potentially infinite and that its focus on factual knowledge
would do little to remedy the supposed effects of advertising itself. In short, the
desirability of some information system akin to an educational provision
would need justification on criteria which had little or no relevance to
advertising. If information regulation is intended, then some direct control on
advertising in its qualitative and quantitative aspects is likely to be the most
fruitful approach, but the scale of advertising and the experience of regulation
suggest that prior compliance with an agreed procedure offers the most sensible
approach. Argument for a direct limitation of expenditure on advertising —
indeed, on all sales promotion — is implicit in the competitive rationale to
which attention is now given.

2.4 Advertising and competition

Economists have paid relatively little attention to the consideration of
advertising as an end in itself and thus the content of advertisements has been of
only peripheral interest, except in regard to information as discussed above.
Greater emphasis has been placed on advertising as a *symptom* of and as a
means to ulterior ends, an approach which may be adequately considered in
terms of the unifying concept of competition.

   A belief or otherwise in competition is a fundamental outcome of a whole
range of intellectual, emotional and experiential sensibilities. The belief need
not be absolute but can be a matter of degree; thus competition can be thought
beneficial in some contexts but not in others and 'too much competition' is as
meaningless as 'too little competition', depending on circumstances. Whilst
competition can be discussed in the abstract, a more useful conceptualisation
proceeds when the precise nature of structure, incentives, information and time
considerations can be defined and the context determined. In common usage,
the term 'a competition' is precisely such a well-defined activity, the eligibility
conditions, rules, duration, means and selection criteria of which are all specified.

A competition typically has formal rules and mores which apply both to the competitors themselves and to any spectators, as in such structured competitions as sports. But less formally structured activities by analogy involve competition where, for example, there is striving for some end which is desirable both in itself and relative to the desires of other competitors, or to an objective standard or to some subjective performance. In these wider contexts the notion of *fair* competition is pervasive but not necessarily independent of self-interest, though there is a presumption that 'fairness' is capable of a general definition in the given context.

The conjunction of the various contexts and the varying perceptions of the incipient rules render the concept of competition capable of innumerable nuances. The use of competition in economics is no exception. As McNulty[21] writes:

'There is probably no concept in all of economics that is at once more funda-mental and pervasive, yet less satisfactorily developed, than the concept of competition.'

Nevertheless, there is a particular abstract conception of competition which is fundamental to economic understanding and whose influence is at the heart of much of economic analysis — 'perfect competition'. The term is used at various levels of aggregation. Thus a firm can be a perfect competitor, in a perfectly competitive industry, in a perfectly competitive system. The essential characteristics of this state of competition are to be seen in both its internal definitions and logic but perhaps more significantly in its methodological position in the structure of economics as a discipline itself, to which McNulty refers above. Certainly both these aspects are inescapable in understanding the general approach to advertising by economists.

However, it is also apparent that the implementation of specific policy provisions, or the appraisal of phenomena against the perspective implicit in the theory of perfect competition by regulatory agencies and the courts must involve an interpretation of those provisions and the tenets upon which they are based in ways that cannot be exclusively or rigorously economic. Neverthe-less, the influence of the model is plainly discernible in the existence and work of such regulatory bodies as the (now defunct) Price Commission, the Monopolies and Mergers Commission and the Office of Fair Trading. Their concern with advertising has, however, been only incidental to wider regulatory concern.

Much confusion is possible if the notion of 'striving' is pursued in connection with the model of perfect competition. Many economic texts, therefore, draw an initial distinction between the businessman's use of 'competition' in this striving sense and the methodological view employed by economists. But confusion is inevitable when economists seek to analyse actual business conduct in terms of a conceptual armoury honed on perfect competition where, for example, adjustment times and transaction costs are ignored. Confusion is compounded when the insights of the analysis of perfect competition are influential (however indirectly) in the determination of policy. The question as to how far this influence extends, even in the context of competition policy, is difficult to answer; how far is advertising policy founded upon the models presented?

The point was made by those eminent scholars, including Clark and Stigler, who produced an official report on the US antitrust laws,[22] that the model of pure/perfect competition is technically constructed in such a way as to have intra-disciplinary significance without indicating ideal conditions for the pursuit of microeconomic policy. They write:[23]

'The concepts of pure and perfect competition are tools of theoretical analysis. They are not intended to and do not constitute a description of reality. As a theoretical model, these ideas give economists means for rigorously exploring the interrelationships of certain specified market forces . . . [T]hey define rigidly the theoretical conditions necessary to a form of long-run equilibrium in which prices would equal costs, including the minimum economically necessary supply price of capital . . .
. . . It should be emphasised that pure and perfect competition are wholly theoretical standards, in that they are not intended *as such* to be guides to public policy.
. . . When taken out of context, the very precision of the theoretical standards of pure and perfect competition can be misleading. Nonetheless, these concepts, used in connection with the study of other factors outside their terms, have helped to orient economists' studies of actual situations, and have contributed, along with other influences, to the elaboration of the theory of workable competition, as an instrument for the direct study of market conditions.'

This compromise position, based upon an implicit, philosophical belief in the benefits of competition, requires that the behaviour of oligopolistic firms be made to conform to that pattern specified in the model of perfect competition even though the appropriate structural conditions are, in reality, unobtainable. But this is very much a compromise because of the 'all or nothing' character of the theory of perfect competition and especially what is known of the theory of second best. In any event, the disposition towards workable competition is explicitly based on perfect competition but, as these economists note:

'There are no objective criteria of workable competition, and such criteria as are proffered are at best intuitively reasonable modifications of the rigorous and abstract criteria of perfect competition.'

Thus the notion of workable competition is no more than:

'a rough and ready judgement by some economists, each for himself, that a particular industry is performing reasonably well.'[24]

Nevertheless, although the precise effects of the advocacy of workable competition by such economists as Clark are a matter for history to judge, the employment of concepts based upon the foundations of perfect competition are undeniably evident from the statements of intent and the interpretations reported in particular cases tried within the framework of competition (anti-trust) policies. The very definition of the terms 'monopoly', 'concentration', 'profit', 'price-fixing', 'collusion', and so on are based essentially upon standards derived from the concept of perfect competition. More specifically, the so-called 'monopoly problem' is defined where there is scope for the existence of prices which depart from marginal cost, where marginal cost is inclusive of all returns necessary to maintain continuity of production. But this conception of marginal cost (in general, both the maximum and minimum cost) as a basis for 'correct' pricing has significance only in the equilibrium and Pareto-optimal conditions associated with perfect competition.[25] In perfect competition, however, there is no advertising: any advertising would necessitate a price in excess of marginal production costs which is unsustainable against the competition. The presence of advertising therefore indicates the non-existence of perfect competition — a state indicative of 'monopoly'. The intellectual justification for the regulation of monopoly is, however, almost certainly based upon *political* assessments of the characteristic nature of industrial and commercial behaviours, which were not contained by the then existing law, e.g. where cartels or mergers led to price discrimination or 'high' prices. As Scherer[26] puts it:

'About the only group in America other than big business outspokenly uncon-cerned about the trust problem were the professional economists.'

Subsequently, the very language of anti-trust and the conceptual framework underpinning it developed a close affinity to that of the perfect competition model. The direct connections among perfect competition — the structure–conduct–performance paradigm which it inspired and the competition policies — remain, however, somewhat obscure. Writing in 1978, Hay and Morris[27] assert that:

'What is not available is a clear presentation of the case for or against inter-vention',

though, of course, intervention via competition policy has been a fact since the late nineteenth century, e.g. in the US Sherman Act of 1890. Economists, nevertheless, have taken the model of perfect competition — which is so central to their education — as the inspiration for the advocacy of competition policy.

It may be concluded, at least by economists (all of whom are educated in the theory of perfect competition) that competition policy is, of necessity, inspired by that model.

Perfect competition is an abstraction which envisages a market that is responsive to the separate requirements of both consumers and producers through the mechanism of a price. Price information is all that consumers need to make optimal purchasing decisions and, relative to their known costs, producers decide how much to produce for given prices. Price responsiveness clears the market so that both consumers and producers achieve the best possible outcomes, the consumers in terms of their own criteria of value and the producers in terms of profit. The competitive aspect arises in so far as only those consumers willing and able to pay the price obtain the good, and any producer's divergence from the price determined by the market overall would lead to pressure to conform. The resultant competition is therefore highly stylised and is tantamount to a state of virtually *no* competition, especially when the market is cleared and the equilibrium price is established, for then there is a conformity between producers and a uniformity of price to consumers and the vestiges of competition apparent in a disequilibrium situation are no longer present.

As much for methodological reasons as for completion of the logical specification of perfect competition, various additional features are typically assumed. Thus the product itself is homogeneous; no producer can offer additional features or create a difference which distinguishes his product from that of any other producer. Accordingly, the consumer is indifferent between suppliers: he cannot obtain any additional value. It is this uniformity in all possible respects which induces compliance to the price signal and which makes price the only determinant of behaviour. The combination of product and price uniformity and the presumption that all participants are informed make the prospect of any advertising redundant on two counts. In the first place, there is no information which is not already known which an advertising message could convey and second, any attempt to advertise would incur costs and so render that advertiser uncompetitive: he would no longer be profitable at the ruling price and so would either have to cease advertising or leave that industry.

Despite the categorical exclusion of advertising from the perfectly competitive scheme, there are analytical currents in other models which do incorporate advertising and which stem directly from the perfectly competitive model. Once there is a relaxation of the assumptions that designate perfect competition, there is scope for a plethora of more complex situations whose analytical characteristics become increasingly difficult to establish. Thus, for methodological reasons rather than to create a more realistic framework, the predominant models with an advertising input are as stylised as the model of perfect competition. Consider, for example, the monopoly model. The monopolist is the sole producer, a profit maximiser with a unique product. His market power is such that he can determine either the quantity to produce and thus establish a price, or, accepting a price, can produce to clear the market at that level. The standard comparison of a monopolist's price and output decision with that of an equivalent perfectly competitive industry — with the same cost structure — demonstrates that the monopolist prices higher and, as a consequence, satisfies a smaller demand. Furthermore, even if he did not profit-maximise, his profitability could be assured by virtue of his market power, since he is insulated from competition as the sole producer of the product. In this situation it is not at all evident why such a monopolist should revert to advertising; he is either in a position where he can maximise profit without advertising, or can obtain satisfactory profit with or without advertising — assuming that the level of advertising expenditure is not so great as to eliminate profit. It may be that if the monopolist does advertise, he can obtain an even greater absolute level of maximum profit, perhaps through the partitioning of his market to take advantage of differences in demand at different places and/or times, but the literature is not forthcoming on the advertising behaviour of the discriminating monopolies. (Note that sole producers of a product may be in competition with the products of other industries — the likelihood of this rises dramatically with levels of consumers' discretionary income — but this possibility is not explicitly incorporated into the monopoly model.) The monopoly model with advertising has been extended in various ways from the basic versions which assume that price and product decisions have been previously made and that only an advertising decision remains; in these extensions price and advertising, on the assumption of a given product, can be jointly determined under the profit-maximising assumption and this methodological approach is easily extendable to incorporate style variations or decisions on product versions.[28] Again, this approach can incorporate a measure of interdependence between competitors (oligopolists), though the sequencing of decisions with respect to the variables and the range of competitive options tends to necessitate drastic simplifications to make the models tractable.

The influence of the methodological devices employed to define perfect competition is further to be seen in the evolution of the more complex models in which advertising conceivably plays some role. Primary interest focuses still upon the various participants' pricing behaviour and there is a determined attempt to standardise, for analytical purposes, as many other variables as possible. With rare exception:

1. The product is taken as given for a particular firm and is assumed to be both responsive to and determined by production costs rather than its qualitative attributes as perceived by consumers.
2. There is a presumed, known demand for that product amongst potential consumers, to which the firm automatically reacts.
3. Price and advertising responses are also known.
4. Decision time and adjustment response by both consumers and competitors are instantaneous.
5. Equilibrium is established nonetheless.
6. Advertising is expressed only in expenditure terms without recognition of its allocation or qualitative dimensions.

7. All costs are known and the assumed sole motivation of the firm is profit
    maximisation.

The models which depart from the assumptions of the perfectly
competitive model are conventionally classified as models of *imperfect
competition*: in view of the constraints imposed by the above assumptions, the
only remaining sphere of emphasis for such models is the production of the
product — in terms of the minimum costs appropriate to a particular output,
dependent upon price. In comparison with the perfect competition model,
these models depict theoretical situations in which the firm has influence over
its price/output decision and in which, accordingly, price diverges from the
marginal cost of production including the normal profit necessary for the
continuation of that production. This failure to produce at marginal cost
indicates both that some reallocation of resources would increase the total
output of goods and that the profitability which derives from the underlying
market power could finance such expenditures as advertising and thereby
insulate the firm's markets from competitive incursion. It is the departure from
marginal-cost pricing that is the hallmark of the various conceptions of
imperfect competition and it is the association of advertising with the state of
imperfect competition that justifies (given the logical basis of those
conceptions) the critical view that traditional theoretical economists take of
advertising. Moreover, while perfect competition provides the theoretical
raison d'être of the structure-conduct-performance paradigm, its empirical
testing has generally been undertaken within the framework supplied by
models of imperfect competition. Perhaps it is this dichotomy which prompts
Nelson's comment[29] that:

'Industrial organisation is a field that is in deep intellectual trouble' [and that]
'the source of that trouble is the old textbook theory that we all know so well.'

The capacity of advertising to distort competition extends in principle to
situations in which advertising is entirely informative, but the usual
presumption is that imperfect competition is generally associated with
'persuasive advertising', though this tends to constitute something of a catch-all
category.

The basic level of analysis has been the industry and insufficient
consideration has been given to the demands of intermediaries in the
distribution channels. The industry focus tends to imply that the product is
homogeneous and from this basis comparisons of costs, rate of return, prices
and profitability ensue whilst advertising is treated purely as a cost without
regard to its qualitative features and its differing roles at the various stages of
distribution. This restricted context, in conjunction with the difficulties in
measuring advertising, has led to a set of generally inconsistent and inconclusive findings that support few generalisations but which do sustain an
enduring controversy, often about technical detail rather than the major thrust

of argument. A more pragmatic approach to the range of results and the welter of arguments follows if one accepts that there are indeed differences in the effectiveness of advertising in some product categories, under certain circumstances at particular times. Thus evidence which shows that nationally branded products have higher prices than own-label unadvertised brands is not, could not and should not be used to 'demonstrate' that advertising raises prices, confers excessive profitability on the advertiser, leads to the exploitation of consumers and disadvantages potential competitors. It *may* contribute to these effects but to ascertain that this is so requires a much fuller analysis of the product characteristics, pricing policies, consumer perceptions, distribution facts, time scale, the number of competitors and their perceptions, as well as such factors as the rate of product obsolesence, the content and management of the advertising itself and all costs. Without such knowledge, there is no prospect of determining the relationships between advertising, pricing and profits. If it could be demonstrated that advertising caused higher prices and profits, then to what implications or conclusions would this lead? To the structure–conduct–performance adherent, it would be proof that advertising is associated with monopoly power, with its deleterious consequences perhaps requiring remedial action. This conclusion, however, can only be based on the comparison with the perfectly competitive model where advertising cannot exist and accordingly the conclusion following from the 'proof' is in fact little more than an affirmation of a belief in the theory that makes the compilation and elaboration of evidence redundant.

The awesome nature of such a conclusion (that any advertising is indicative of monopoly power) is tempered by the delineation of circumstances where some advertising is or can be beneficial. This is attempted by the separation of advertising into what are seen as mutually exclusive categories — persuasive advertising and informational advertising — and a further correlation of a predominance of either of these forms with specific market conditions. Thus persuasive advertising with negligible information content is thought to be typical of oligopolistic markets with relatively mature products, whilst in new product introductions — especially for innovatory products — informative advertising prevails. In other terms, informative advertising has a constructive role to fulfil, whilst persuasive advertising is almost invariably suspect. Information, especially that relating to price, could be viewed as essential to the actual operation of markets (there was a lack of appreciation of this prior to Stigler's 1961 paper on the economics of information[30]), but the standard economics approach has been to consider the benefits of information relative to its cost, under the assumption that both of these are known — which is a partial view of information because it presumes not only that the extent of ignorance is known but also that the value of information is always knowable in advance. The role of information as the lubricant for the smooth-working of the market mechanism, and its treatment as a good which in turn is analysable in terms of price ensure that a restricted view is taken of the potential role of information. Again this is to confine its analysis within traditional bounds. For instance, the logical probability that information alone could lead to a change in perception of the merits of a good is typically described as persuasion changing tastes and the primacy of an initial set of tastes which remain constant is a *sine qua non* of economic reasoning. In this manner, only certain forms of information are accorded explicit attention and the ways in which information is circulated and used is circumscribed. The consumer knows his own tastes but an information mechanism to redress forgetting, for instance, must be precluded because forgetting could also apply to tastes; moreover, the explicit demand for something that is forgotten is impossible and such a 'market' would defy economic analysis — at least in conventional terms.

The role of advertising in indicating the supply of information on prices leading to a lower level of prices for specific goods has been documented, e.g. by Benham,[31] Steiner,[32] Farris and Albion.[33] Advertised information has also been credited as an indirect signal of product quality and reputation, irrespective of the qualitative content of advertisements, (see Nelson[34]). These aspects have made little impression on the traditional view that advertising, at least in the quantities typically used, is a determinant and symptom of market power and that the informational aspects are dwarfed into insignificance by the blatant attempt at persuasion. In the absence of market expansion, this advertising merely divides market share between advertisers and represents a socially-egregious use of resources. Where consumers are already informed by repetitive advertising and differentiated products are essentially similar, any benefits to consumers from induced switching between products or in being persuaded to maintain a particular purchase pattern are even in aggregate, small compared to the sums expended on advertising. This 'fact', it is believed, is also recognised by some advertisers themselves who would welcome a reduction of advertising expenses in favour of more constructive or productive use of funds. They are, however, locked into the advertising system by two considerations. First, a unilateral reduction or withdrawal of advertising would risk loss of competitive position *vis-à-vis* existing producers and, secondly, it would make that product market more accessible to new competitors. Moreover, consumers, too, would be likely to favour less-confusing advertising and reduced prices persisting into the longer term rather than being subjected to advertised price reductions on a sporadic basis. The prevalence of this argument is to be seen in the approach of the official bodies involved with monopolies control and price policy over recent years. For instance:

'The consumer would benefit if the area of competition on price could be increased at the expense, if need be, either of outlays on advertising and promotion or of profit.'[35]

'But advertising which merely seeks to expand one seller's market share at the expense of other sellers' shares is likely to be partly self-cancelling and the overall unit cost of unchanging output is then likely to be higher than it would be with a smaller expenditure on advertising. Such an increase in unit costs would represent a waste of resources and would constitute a serious public interest issue.'[36]

'Advertising has been directed mainly towards establishing brand image; informative advertising which aids the consumer has played a minor role. This marketing strategy, based on strong brand loyalty and reinforced by heavy advertising and promotional expenditure, adds to costs. We accept that in recent years advertising has included a growing element of information to consumers but nonetheless, the overall marketing strategy continues to be designed to build up brand loyalty and thus it restricts competition.'[37]

'. . . various forms of entry barrier have been uncovered by the Monopolies and Mergers Commission which found they were against the public interest . . . A high level of expenditure on advertising or other sales promotion will also act to discourage new entrants.'[38]

In the USA, the FTC[39] has adopted a similar view, notably in the recent case against the ready-to-eat breakfast cereal producers where the four major producers were *inter alia* charged that:

'these practices of proliferating brands, differentiating similar products and promoting trade marks through intensive advertising result in high barriers to entry into the RTE cereal market'.

2.5 Conclusions

Economically-oriented public policy towards advertising is influenced to a major degree by the implications drawn from the conventional theoretical structures relating individually and in combination to consumer behaviour, to perfect and imperfect competition and to informative and persuasive advertising. Of tangential interest only has been concern with blatant misrepresentation and falsity; centre stage has been held by quantitative expenditures on advertising, and the circumstances which have enabled firms to advertise and the subsequent effects on prices — via various routes, e.g. concentration, entry exclusion, etc. Advertising, as both a determinant and a symptom of monopolistic structures, has been considered primarily in the wider context of the policy and procedure for the regulation of monopoly. Although this machinery is brought to bear only selectively by the relevant authorities against particular practices in certain industries, it is indisputable that a climate, or a more generic policy orientation, is exhibited by these cases. Indeed, traditional economics can be seen as part of the foundation of the EEC draft Directive (see Chapter 1) and more extensively in the general debate on advertising control. Qualifications to the traditional view are present in economics literature but these have had little influence on policy.

There is a determination to employ the model of perfect competition as if it had some connotation as an ideal state and as if it provided a logical basis for the analysis of advertising. This is seen in the equation of advertising with the derogatory category of imperfect competition; also, in the identification of cases where a supposedly informative function is excluded and advertising is classified as persuasive. But perfect competition is neither ideal nor does it provide a logical basis for the analysis of advertising. Indeed, placing advertising in the domain of imperfectly competitive models, as conventionally constructed, leaves economics with remarkably little to offer which is relative specifically to advertising. Thus, concluding a recent review of advertising and competition policy, Comanor and Wilson[40] state:

'What is therefore required is a systematic approach towards appraising the gains to consumers from the information contained in advertising. In what circumstances might these gains be large and in what circumstances might they be small or absent entirely? While arguments have been made regarding this issue, there remains no accepted theoretical basis for dealing with questions of this type.'

These authors, in a preceding passage, however, do claim that the *empirical* literature shows:

'That heavy advertising does contribute to high levels of market power in some industries [but] The presence of market failure due to advertising provides no rationale for policy actions unless the specific measures proposed can be demonstrated as superior to the operation of the unfettered market'.

This conclusion on the role of theory is also drawn by Needham:[41] 'economic theory provides no clear guidelines for public policy towards advertising itself', but he sees the empirical evidence on the relationship between advertising and monopoly power as 'scarce and by no means conclusive'. Underlying the quest for empirical evidence in this area is the structure–conduct–performance paradigm which, as we have seen, is dominated by the model of perfect competition. Much of the controversy about empirical conclusiveness and/or inconclusiveness stems ultimately from interpretating the significance of results in the light of this model. Thus, despite the logical irrelevance of perfect competition to advertising, the model is indirectly influential both upon the manner in which empirical investigation is conducted and upon the ultimate judgement of the evidence. Whilst the structure–conduct–performance paradigm is meant to be neither a descriptively realistic model nor an ideal structure, its use is in contradiction of both these aspects, especially where there is the added dimension of the informational aspect of advertising to be considered. The difficulties arise because in a literal sense *any* departure from the theoretical requirements of perfect competition renders it inappropriate, yet substantial departures are regarded as if they were insignificant to the integrity of the model as a whole. The departure from the absolute standard introduces scope for the arbitrary evaluation of economic relationships. To the extent that the very *existence* of advertising is incompatible with perfect competition, the comparison of advertising's performance by the standards derived from that model are inappropriate both *in toto* and in part. Yet the literature exhibits marvellous inventiveness in preserving the perfectly competitive model as the basis for piecemeal and aggregate analyses of advertising. The structuring of enquiry into advertising involves asking such questions as 'does advertising raise prices, increase profit, industry concentration, restrict competitive entry?', all of which invite the question 'from what?' i.e. 'from what standard?' Implicitly, that standard is (almost always) the benchmark conception of perfectly competitive prices equated to marginal costs; perfectly competitive industry equilibrium in respect of profit distributions being uniform and entry and exit being free. Detachment from this standard leaves very little for economists *per se* to prescribe for the structure of industry.

Significantly, the counter arguments employed in defence of alternative visions of competition have generally not been effective against the prevailing economics conception. It is not obvious why this should be the case when the theoretical underpinnings of the perfectly competitive system are so conspicuously absent in the practical contexts reviewed against it. On the other hand, with respect to less technical and formal conceptions of competition (e.g. 'the rat race', 'competitive jungle', *laissez faire*) the integrated and widely endorsed view of perfect competition in the way in which it is applied, serves as a consistent and commercially impartial set of rules by which competitive activity can be judged. Against this set of rules advertising is, and indeed will be, found wanting. To expect otherwise is to mistake both the position of perfect competition in the formal structure of economics and the influence of economics on the formulation of policy towards commerce and industry.

This economic perspective is necessarily partial and incomplete as an economic perspective is but a part of a more comprehensive view. We defer discussion of our own policy conclusions until more detailed consideration of the behaviour of producers and consumers has been undertaken. In Chapter 3 the alternative economic conception of the Austrian school is discussed.

References

1. Cohen, J. 'Psychology and Philosophy of Advertising', in Wilson, A. (ed.), *Advertising and the Community*, Manchester: Manchester University Press, 1968, p.6.
2. For further discussion and examples see Katouzian, M. A. H., *Ideology and Method of Economics*, London: Macmillan, 1980.
3. For an introduction to the issues discussed here, see McKenzie, R. B., 'The Necessary Normative Context of Positive Economists', and Samuels, W. J., 'A Necessary Normative Context of Positive Economics?', both in *Journal of Economic Issues*, vol. 15, no. 3, 1981, pp.703–27.

4. Needham, D., *The Economics of Industrial Structure, Conduct and Performance*, New York: Holt, Rinehart and Winston, 1978, p.264.
5. Comanor, W. S. and Wilson, J. A., 'The Effect of Advertising on Competition: A Survey', *Journal of Economic Literature*, vol. 18, no. 3, 1979, p.451.
6. *Ibid.*, pp.470–472.
7. Block, H., 'The Effect of Advertising on Competition: Comments on a Survey', *Journal of Economic Literature*, vol. 18, no. 4, 1980, pp.1063–78.
8. Machlup, F., 'Liberalism and the Choice of Freedoms', in Streissler, E. (ed.), *Roads to Freedom*, Essays in Honour of Friedrich A. Hayek, London: Routledge and Kegan Paul, 1969.
9. Chiplin, B. and Sturgess, B., *Economics of Advertising*, Second Edition, London: Holt, Rinehart and Winston, with the Advertising Association, 1981.
10. *Ibid.*, p.134.
11. Albion, M. S. and Farris, P. W., *The Advertising Controversy*, Boston, Mass.: Auburn House Publishing Co., 1981, p.30.
12. See, for instance, Scherer, F. M., *Industrial Market Structure and Economic Performance*, Chicago: Rand McNally, 1980, or Needham, D., *op.cit.*
13. Kaldor, N., 'The Economic Aspects of Advertising', *Review of Economic Studies*, vol. 18, 1950, pp.1–27.
14. Meade, J. E., *The Intelligent Radical's Guide to Economic Policy*, London: Allen and Unwin, 1975.
15. Reekie, W. D., 'The Market in Advertising', in Hirst, I. R. C. and Reekie, W. D. (eds.), *The Consumer Society*, London: Tavistock, 1977.
16. Meade, J. E., *Efficiency, Equality and the Ownership of Property*, London: Allen and Unwin, 1964, p.12.
17. Kaldor, N., *op.cit.*, p.7.
18. Resnik, A. and Stern, B. L., 'An Analysis of Information Content in Television Advertising', *Journal of Marketing*, vol. 41, Jan. 1977, pp.50–3.
19. Daly, J. C. (Moderator), *Advertising and the Public Interest*, Washington D.C.: Center for Research on Advertising, American Enterprise Institute for Public Policy Research, 1976, p.5.
20. Meade, J. E., 1975, *op.cit.*, p.49.
21. McNulty, P. J., 'Economic Theory and the Meaning of Competition', *Quarterly Journal of Economics*, vol. 82, 1968.
22. *Report of the Attorney General's National Committee to Study the Antitrust Laws*, Washington D.C.: U.S. Government Printing Office, 1955.
23. *Ibid.*, pp.337–8. Quoted by Liebhafsky, H. H., *The Nature of Price Theory*, Homewood, Ill.: Dorsey, 1963, p.12.
24. *Ibid.*, p.339. Quoted by Liebhafsky, *ibid.*, pp.12–13. See also Hay, D. A. and Morris, D. J., *Industrial Economics*, Oxford: Oxford University Press, 1979, pp.559–65.
25. See, for example, Hay, D. D. and Morris, D. J., *op.cit.*, ch. 16.
26. Scherer, F. M., *op.cit.*, p.493.
27. Hay, D. A. and Morris, D. J., *op.cit.*, p.539.

28. Koutsoyiannis, A., *Non Price Decisions*, London: Macmillan, 1982.
29. Nelson, R. R., 'Goldschmid, Mann, and Weston's Industrial Concentration: The New Learning—A review', *Bell Journal of Economics*, vol. 7, no. 2, Autumn 1976, p.332.
30. Stigler, G. J., 'The Economics of Information', *Journal of Political Economy*, **69**, June 1961, pp.213–225.
31. Benham, L., 'The Effect of Advertising on the Price of Eyeglasses', *Journal of Law and Economics*, vol. **15**, no. 2, 1972, pp.337–52.
32. Steiner, R. L., 'Does Advertising Lower Consumer Prices?', *Journal of Marketing*, vol. **37**, no. 4, Oct. 1973.
33. Farris, P. W. and Albion, M. S., 'The Impact of Advertising on the Price of Consumer Products', *Journal of Marketing*, vol. **44**, Summer 1980, pp.17–35.
34. Nelson, P., 'Advertising as Information', *Journal of Political Economy*, July-August 1974, pp.729–54.
35. National Board for Prices and Incomes, *'Prices of Household and Toilet Soaps, Soap Powders and Soap Flakes and Soapless Detergents'*, Cmnd. 2791, HMSO 1965, para. 65.
36. Monopolies and Mergers Commission, *'Parallel Pricing'*, Cmnd. 5330, HMSO 1973, para. 77.
37. Price Commission, *'Southalls (Birmingham) Ltd., Sanitary Protection and other Hygiene Products'*, H.C. 436, HMSO 1978, para. 2.11.
38. *Review of Monopolies and Mergers Policy: A Consultative Document*, Cmnd. 7198, HMSO 1978, p.3.44.
39. FTC v. Kellogg *et al*, Docket No. 8883, quoted in Schalensee, R., 'Entry Deterrence in the Ready to Eat Breakfast Cereal Industry', *Bell Journal of Economics*, vol. **9**, no. 2, 1975, pp.305–327.
40. Comanor, W. S. and Wilson, J. A., *op.cit.*, p.473.
41. Needham, D., *op.cit.*, p.265.

3

Advertising and Austrian economics

3.1 Introduction

Chapter 2 considered the relationship between economics and advertising policy and demonstrated the part which particular conceptions of both competition and information have traditionally played both in the methodological development of the economics of advertising and in fashioning implications for policy. The influence of this mode of economic thought is not confined, however, to the specific issue of competition policy but extends, somewhat indirectly, into the regulatory rationale and practices discussed hitherto, though there is an inevitable contrast between the two approaches. Chapter 1 emphasised the interpretation and assessment of the qualitative characteristics of advertising whilst the economic approach so far presented has considered advertising almost symbolically with an orientation towards its quantitative characteristics and its very existence. In this chapter these two separate orientations — broadly, the qualitative and quantitative — are partially reconciled in the economic analysis of advertising of the Austrian school. This approach stems from the emphasis placed on a subjectivist approach to economic behaviour, with individualistic assessment of phenomena and thus with closer attention to the perceived realities that impinge both on advertisers and the consumer. This in turn leads to an alternative conception of the role of advertising in the competitive process from which different policy prescriptions ensue.

It is only recently that the characteristic approach of the Austrian school has found a wider audience and there are no extended discussions and few citations to the approach in advertising literature, although a more general introduction to Austrian thought is found in Kirzner[1] and Littlechild.[2] Accordingly, it is appropriate here to give some insight into the microeconomic methodology of this school and to note points of similarity and difference with the more familiar neo-classical (or mainstream) approach which largely underpins the discussion in the previous chapters. At some risk of over-simplifying the Austrian contribution to the topic, the major features of their analysis are briefly summarised in the context of advertising.

For a variety of reasons, Austrians elucidate a conception of competition as a *process* rather than the *state* assumed by the perfect competition model. The Austrian conception attaches greater significance to the roles of time and uncertainty in perpetuating disequilibrium in markets, even though there may be some equilibratory tendencies. The comparative imperfection of markets does not imply that they will continue to exhibit such features and analysis of the history of market structures shows them to be susceptible to change. From this perspective, advertising is not necessarily to be seen as antithetical to competition, more as an essential part of it. Thus any of the conventional criticisms of advertising arising from the static theory of imperfect competition may be reversed: for instance, advertising may facilitate competitive entry rather than impede it; the association of advertising with supra-normal profitability is redundant; advertising rather than being socially wasteful of resources can be socially beneficial; moreover the Austrians consider the orthodox distinction between selling costs and production costs as arbitrary and in the face of information requirements and information clutter, persuasion is necessary to impart information.

This approach, it will immediately be appreciated, is similar to the views of advertising held by the business community and marketing theorists, views which have been consistently at variance with those of mainstream economists who have remained impervious to them. Ultimately, the choice between contrasting approaches to advertising generates considerable emotion — but the limited choice between Austrian and mainstream economic analysis may initially be expounded in terms of logic alone.

3.2 Essentials of the Austrian perspective

The school of Austrian economists employs many of the standard concepts of conventional neo-classical economics but certain concepts receive a greater emphasis and, by a cumulation of often subtle distinctions, the overall integrated approach to microeconomics is in some respects dramatically different. Some indication of the differences between the two methodologies is shown by the following extract from Kirzner:[3]

'The general outline of the Austrian position on methodology is well known. Austrian economists are subjectivists; they emphasise the purposefulness of human action; they are unhappy with constructions that emphasise. equilibrium to the exclusion of market processes; they are deeply suspicious of attempts to apply measurement procedures to economics; they are sceptical of empirical "proofs" of economic theorems and consequently have serious reservations about the validity and importance of a good deal of the empirical work being carried on in the economics profession today.'

The subject matter of all economics is human action where this is purposeful rather than reflex action; accordingly attention is centred on the individual's

perception of alternatives. However, due recognition has to be given to unique-
ness of the individual for it is apparent from introspection and observation that
the guiding force of action — the motivation of the individual — resides solely
with him; indeed, the objective world only assumes meaning through the
individual's mental activity and purposes. The individual's inevitable confrontation with alternatives amongst which he is impelled by purposefulness to
choose, serves to define the scope of economics and thus:[4]

'The recognition of purposefulness is, of course, fundamental to our definition
of economics as the logic of choice.'

The alternatives which arise in any context of choice are known or knowable
only by the individual. When a choice is made, it follows that the displaced
categories of purposeful action are not realised since it is these which are always
rejected. The only person who can assess the nature of these alternatives is the
individual himself who will perceive them according to a unique mental state
and at a unique moment in time. The best displaced alternative is the
'opportunity cost' — hereafter 'cost' — which is necessarily subjective. Cost is
therefore a concept specific to an individual, it exists only in his mind and is an
ex ante concept which expires at the moment of decision or choice.[5] What is
observable to the individual or to others, are the consequences or outcomes of
the choices made. These outcomes may be the realisation of *ex ante* conjectures
by the individual but, because the future is inherently uncertain, the outcomes
do not necessarily conform to expectations. The outcomes may well impinge
upon other people: the consequences of an individual's choice could be to the
benefit or detriment of these other people. However, any cost would remain
unknowable since it would only arise at the moment when these people each
make a decision involving choice, displacing their alternatives which
accordingly are unrealised.

In neo-classical economics, the term 'opportunity cost' is defined in terms of
a displaced alternative but its usage is not in line with a thoroughgoing subjectivist interpretation. Rather, in the case of a purchase for instance, the 'cost'
is assumed to be the monetary value of alternative expenditure, that is, the
money itself. Thus 'opportunity costs' become measurable money costs and
subjectivity is replaced by objectivity. Whilst, of course, it is true that money
spent on A precludes its expenditure on B, the cost is the *value* forgone in displacing B which may extend beyond the monetary dimension. Money and
prices, expressed in monetary units, are but data and contributory inputs to a
decision. However, they only assume meaning in the context of a decision
although a choice involves more than the displacement of mere money, so
money cannot be the totality of an alternative and therefore it is not a cost. In
discussing whether subjective costs can be represented by objectively-measured
outlays on goods and factors, Vaughn[6] argues that the subjective evaluations of
forgone opportunities are equal to prices only in 'full timeless certain general

equilibrium'. It is precisely because the Austrians stress the importance of time, the inherent uncertainty surrounding decisions and the conception of the *process* towards, rather than the state of, equilibrium, that this relationship is of little importance except as a 'useful fiction' on a 'pedagogical level'.[7] In neo-classical economics, however, 'the full timeless certain general equilibrium' is of prime importance principally because it may be shown theoretically that a perfectly competitive system would under certain assumptions achieve such an equilibrium and, moreover, that modern welfare economics takes this equilibrium as the basis for policy recommendations involving competition policy. Indeed, the censorius view of imperfect competition and thus of advertising stems from this core result.

That such a full equilibrium is impossible to achieve derives from failure for equilibria in sub-systems to be sufficiently extensive due to problems of timing and uncertainty. Any decision-maker may well have his anticipations and expectations confounded by events including the actions of others. What Hayek[8] calls the 'unintended consequences of human action' perpetuate an unceasing sequence of decisions as action and reaction proceed. Furthermore, as Lachmann[9] states, the changing state of knowledge that is inherent in the 'passage of time' prompts fresh decisions and perpetuates this process and the stream of knowledge produces ever new disequilibrium situations. For both the individual and others the unexpected consequences of human action, the consequences of the unforeseeable and the unforeseen present the necessity of further decisions. Plans must be adapted and actions reconsidered in a series of unique circumstances. How the individual performs these actions in his ability to perceive the need, formulate alternatives and adapt to change is not itself unchanging. The alertness of the individual to those circumstances and actions which better serve his self-interest is a key factor in the Austrian conception of 'entrepreneurship' which describes the complex of abilities which the individual deploys in a decision. As Kirzner[10] puts it:

'It is the entrepreneurial element that is responsible for our understanding of human action as active, creative and human rather than as passive, automatic and mechanical.'

But an individual's action on his own exclusive behalf accounts for only a part of the totality of his actions. The purposes which he serves and the roles he plays depend also upon the context of his decisions. For instance, the role of the individual in such an institution as a firm, where others too serve ends originating from exterior sources, raises complex issues if both subjectivism and a methodological individualistic approach are to be maintained. Nevertheless, the Austrian conception of a firm requires that entrepreneurship can be exhibited and that this is necessarily by an individual whether or not he is part of a group.

The motivation of the individual is *profit* which is variously defined by

Austrian writers. A comprehensive and subjectivist interpretation of the term is given by von Mises:[11]

'Action is an attempt to substitute a more satisfactory state of affairs for a less satisfactory one. We call such a wilfully induced alteration an exchange. A less desirable condition is bartered for a more desirable. What gratifies less is abandoned in order to attain something that pleases more. That which is abandoned is called the price paid for the attainment of the end sought. The value of the price paid is called costs. Costs are equal to the value attached to the satisfaction which one must forego in order to attain the end aimed at. The difference between the value of the price paid (the costs incurred) and that of the goal attained is called gain or profit or net yield. Profit in this primary sense is purely subjective, it is an increase in acting man's happiness, it is a psychical phenomenon that can be neither measured nor weighed . . . Only the ordinal numbers can be applied to it, but not the cardinal numbers.'

From this definition of profit it follows that an individual, whether in a firm or not, is posited at the point of decision concerned with the maximisation of profit, for the individual takes the best of the options as he perceives them. Because there is no basis for the rejection of the 'best' except to supplant it with a newly perceived 'best' which is in its turn 'the best', the proposition that profit is maximised is self-evidently true and 'is implied in the very category of action'. Despite their subjective interpretation of the term 'profit', both von Mises and others also employ it in the conventional, objective sense of the difference between objective costs and revenue. However, a distinctive Austrian aspect is exhibited in the linking of profit to entrepreneurship:

'Like any acting man the entrepreneur is always a speculator. He deals with the uncertainties of the future . . . The only source from which an entre- preneur's profits stem is his ability to anticipate better than other people the future demand of consumers.'[12]

The use of the word 'only' here requires elaboration; it specifically means that pure entrepreneurial profit is not related to ownership but arises from 'the dis- covery of something available for nothing at all',[13] which is the return to the alertness shown in detecting and benefiting from the difference between a buying opportunity and a selling one. A market process is dependent on the profit motivation of the entrepreneur. According to Lachmann:[14]

'Entrepreneurs continually manage to find new price-cost differences to exploit. When one is eliminated by strenuous competition, the stream of knowledge throws up another. Profit is the permanent income from ever changing sources',

and von Mises[15] states:

'In eliminating the entrepreneur one eliminates the driving force of the whole market system'.

From this brief description it is apparent that the twin pillars of the Austrian position are the requirement that economic analysis should be concerned with individuals — methodological individualism — and that accordingly the basis of analysis should be their subjective valuations of alternatives prior to action — subjectivism. It is from this basis that the fullest and most realistic factors that actually comprise human decision-making must be recognised. This is in contrast to those approaches which maintain unrealistic assumptions for ulterior reasons and which seek to reduce the diversity which is undeniable in individuals to a stylised model.

The entrepreneur-based Austrian conception of competition has the features of uncertainty, rivalry, speculative activity and reaction and is in sharp contrast to the term competition in 'perfect competition', because the assumptions of the model emasculate 'competitors' so that only conformity is possible. Product homogeneity, perfect knowledge and price uniformity are an equilibrium state which is the antithesis of a market process featuring the perpetual jockeying for advantage. The assumptions of the state of perfect competition preclude the search for comparative advantage in terms of product feature, place and (ultimately) price, whereas the entrepreneur in a rivalrous process will seek to exploit any superiority of knowledge or perception through action.

3.3 Austrian views on advertising

A broad overview of the Austrian position on advertising may be obtained from the writings of von Mises. Later writers — notably Kirzner — have refined the rather sweeping assertions of von Mises and related them in more detail to the general methodological stance of the Austrians, but the overall tenor of the conclusions remains the same. Von Mises is quoted at some length but the later elaboration owes much to the work of Kirzner.

von Mises

Von Mises uses the term 'business propaganda' synonymously with advertising and defines its general purpose in terms of information. The consumer's lack of information on price, product availability and product suitability (amongst other things) leaves him at best with his past experiences of market conditions as his means of removing the 'particular uneasiness he wants to remove':

'To convey to him information about the actual state of the market is the task of business propaganda.'[16]

He is highly critical of the form and presentation of advertising rather than of the messages themselves. He holds elitist views and clearly believes that what he considers bad advertising will crowd out the good — Gresham's law applied to advertising rather than Elizabethan coins. Thus he writes:

'Business propaganda must be obtrusive and blatant. It is its aim to attract the attention of slow people; to rouse latent wishes, to entice men to substitute innovation for inert clinging to traditional routine. In order to succeed, advertising must be adjusted to the mentality of the people courted. It must suit their tastes and speak their idiom. Advertising is shrill, noisy, coarse, puffing, because the public does not react to dignified allusions. It is the bad taste of the public that forces the advertisers to display bad taste in their publicity campaigns. The art of advertising has evolved into a branch of applied psychology, a sister discipline of pedagogy.
'Like all things designed to suit the taste of the masses, advertising is repellent to people of delicate feeling.'[17]

He views advertising recipients as a 'jury': the various advertising claims are like the statements of witnesses which, with other evidence, may contribute to a decision. The advertising messages themselves do not provide a means for making the consumer buy whatever the advertiser wants them to buy; moreover, even the 'gullible public' is unlikely to be cheated by the 'tricks and artifices' of advertising for long because satisfaction with the product on purchase is essential and poor choices will not be repeated. Indeed, he thinks there is a consensus amongst businessmen that in the end it is only good products which are worth advertising. However, the bulk of advertising is for frequently-bought consumer goods which are by definition the subject of repeat purchase.

Von Mises states that there are some notorious and persistent examples of products which are offered to exploit the gullible, of which patent medicine is the most cited. Although the 'sad fact that some people try to exploit their fellow man's plight', would seem more an indictment of man rather than of the means employed, advertisements for such products frequently offend. These advertisements and those which mislead or 'induce a man to try an article which he would not have bought if he had known its qualities beforehand' are, of course, paid sponsorship and the public should beware. Nevertheless, recipients may still suffer. But people may act for many reasons in ways they ultimately regret, so to isolate the responsibility of advertising is a problem. To those who would proscribe advertising in the cases of conspicuous abuse von Mises[18] cautions that:

'Freedom is indivisible. As soon as one starts to restrict it, one enters upon a decline on which it is difficult to stop. If one assigns to the government the task of making truths prevail in the advertising of perfumes and toothpaste, one cannot contest it the right to look after the truth in the more important matters of religion, philosophy, and social ideology.'

Of the assertion that:

'Advertising and all other methods of business propaganda are condemned as one of the most outrageous outgrowths of unlimited competition'[19] von Mises does not offer a direct detailed critique. However, in the absence of governmental regulation the control of excessive advertising rests with the self-interest of the advertiser. The businessman will only employ advertising so far as his net proceeds are expected to increase. Advertising then is subject to the same controls as other business costs.

'In this regard there is no difference between the costs of advertising and all other costs of production.'[20]

Overall, von Mises is concerned with only the general nature and effects of advertising. His treatment is brief, characteristically forceful, wide-ranging but only loosely related to a specifically economic approach. Development of some of his insights, however, and a wider integration of the Austrian view are contained in the work of Kirzner.

Kirzner

There are various strands to Kirzner's discussion of advertising, but a co-ordinating theme is its relationship to entrepreneurship and hence to the competitive process. His treatment of the subject[21] relies on lengthy comparisons with the neo-classical view and revolves round two pervasive dichotomies: selling and production costs, and information and persuasion. His overall positions may be summarised as follows.

Advertising as communication is employed by entrepreneurs in their attempts to make the consumer aware of the opportunities which the entrepreneur provides. This must, however, be distinguished from the separate function of providing information. Recognition that (advertised) information is not necessarily separable from the product involves consideration of product definition and whether the advertising is persuasive or informative. Persuasion can increase consumer eagerness for an existing product, help rectify the consequences of previous entrepreneurial mistakes or correct consumers' mistaken views. Furthermore, persuasion is necessary in getting the consumer to 'notice' the opportunity and, as such, advertising is a normal competitive activity. With the conception of competition as a process rather than an equilibrium state, quite different implications emerge for the role of advertising and its contribution to society. Furthermore, the paradox that advertising is both a result of an excess of competition in some contexts and a symptom of lack of competition in others is resolved if competition is seen as rivalry.

In elaborating his position it is necessary to consider the nature of a product and the traditional distinction between selling and production costs which, following Chamberlin, has been at the centre of definitions of imperfect competition. (Perfect competition is defined exclusively in terms of production costs so selling costs, even for the provision of information, are axiomatically precluded.) The entrepreneur, in a competitive process, attempts to offer to consumers 'something they seek eagerly' and the dimensions of this attraction can extend beyond price. Accordingly, a market disequilibrium can be defined in terms of an entrepreneurial attempt to discover the appropriate combination of product features, price, information and location, all of which effectively comprise the 'product'. That some of these dimensions are conventional selling costs, because they do not refer to a homogeneous physical product, demonstrates the arbitrary definition of 'product' in the neo-classical models and, given that all participants are not endowed with perfect information, it is part of the entrepreneurial function to alert consumers not only to the 'product' but also to its desirability. Indeed the entrepreneur must not only disseminate information or knowledge but he must also engage in 'relieving the consumer of the necessity to be his own entrepreneur'.

On the definition of a product, conventional theory has usually been content to accept it as given, along with the conveniently defined industry which produces it. In this scheme, product quality and the mix of associated utilities of place and information are not explicitly recognised. However, even Chamberlin[22] found difficulty in maintaining the separate definition of a product and ensuring that production and selling costs could remain distinct, especially in the case of advertising:

'A question might be raised as to certain types of advertising which add prestige to a product, or which in one way or another lead to greater appreciation on the part of those who buy it and own it. Although it is the result of advertising, such added 'utility' might be considered a part of the product and therefore a cost of production in the sense that every buyer gets it even if some care nothing about it. We seem to have merely another example of one element of a composite product which the buyer gets even though he would rather not pay for it.'

In general, however, Chamberlin takes the product — the outcome of production, not selling, activities — as given and only subsequently considers the role of selling costs including advertising. The distinction, he maintained, was essential to separate those activities which bring a product into being and those that affect demand for it. But, if the product is a 'variable' and is variable in many dimensions according to the perception of the entrepreneur who sees a potential demand for some composite set of attributes, then the expenditure incurred in organising a product in line with this anticipated demand comprises both categories of production and selling costs. Yet this separation of costs is not possible — they are all selling costs in the sense that a product is created which will sell. Alternatively, in a logical sense they are all production costs since in combination they contribute to the product and are all ingredients in the attempt by the entrepreneur to meet a demand. In short, the selling cost/production cost distinction is invalid.

The entrepreneurial task involves making the consumer aware of the product, which entails more than simply providing the consumer with knowledge to make him buy the product . The significance of this distinction stems from the nature of information assumed in the traditional consumer model: here, the knowledge of prices and products is sufficient for the mechanistic calculation of product combinations which give the consumer the greatest utility. But in an entrepreneurial system the consumer might not 'see' the full range of potential calculations open to him. It is to the benefit of entre-preneurs to get such consumers to see and know of the opportunities available to them. But this is not attempted only *after* a product has been created, rather the process of product creation will involve recognition and inclusion of those attributes of which the consumer either is or can be made aware. In respect of timing, the distinction between selling and production costs is invalid.

Turning to advertising, Kirzner addresses the enduring distinction between information and persuasion. He notes that those writers, notably Hicks and Chamberlin, who had little sympathy with the distinction nevertheless saw the information—whether persuasive in character or not—as separate from the product. Kirzner concedes that this may possibly be the case:[23]

'Let it immediately be conceded that a substantial portion of advertising may indeed, as the cited literature argues, be viewed as providing a service quite distinct from the advertised product . . . what I wish to point out is simply to treat *all* informational aspects of advertising *exclusively* as providing a separate distinct service ("information") fails utterly to perceive the crucially important role of the entrepreneur as one who *brings available opportunities to the* awareness of the consumer.'

But the conventional analysis of advertising employing the demand curve — in which advertising as separate information shifts an existing demand curve to the right — is inadequate when the information is not separate from, but *is* the product and necessary even to *establish* the demand curve:

'that is, it consists of messages making the consumer aware of unknown commodities or of unperceived desirable qualities of already known commodities.'[24]

Clearly, if the product is not perceived, there can be no readiness to pay (any price) either for the product itself or the information:

'providing information turns out to be essential in order to attach meaning to the general notion that a demanded product exists.'[25]

The persuasive nature of much, if not most, advertising must be accounted for because it is not obvious why the entrepreneur should be engaged in persuasion rather than more careful attention to consumer desires in the first instance. The explanation Kirzner gives is that persuasion may be necessary to retrieve entrepreneurial mistakes and 'avoid the abandonment and waste of efforts and resources already invested' or to make consumers more eager for a product they already desire. However, as many have noted, something more than 'bleak' information is required to gain the notice of consumers and persuasion is required for effective communication. And so:

'greater and greater portions of entrepreneurial effort and alertness are
dedicated to discovering ways to communicate with consumers'

with the result that:

'the superficial observer of advertising in an affluent society will perceive a
smaller relative information content in its advertising messages than is found
in less affluent societies'.[26]

But advertising competition in getting the consumer to be aware of a particular product could be so successful that a temporary monopoly position is established. This may be the outcome of entrepreneurial alertness in general and, although a particular advertising message may be unique, the potential for other messages in combination with product characteristics is infinite. Freedom to create alternative advertising messages is not denied by a single advertiser but the delay involved in a suitable creation could sustain temporary monopoly. In general, however, Kirzner believes that advertising is fully consistent with an entrepreneurial competitive process — indeed, it is a necessary component of it, especially in the disequilibrium conditions that prevail. The apparent duplication or waste that occurs in competitive advertising, which is the result of a trial and error attempt by separate entrepreneurs to fulfil demand, is revealed by the market outcome and could not be known beforehand and it reflects the imperfection of knowledge that necessarily appertains in the economy.

'In calling such duplication wasteful one is presumably passing judgement
from the perspective of assumed omniscience.'[27]

Extension

It is fair to state that Kirzner's — and indeed von Mises's — treatment of advertising is peripheral to the main points they wished to make. Accordingly, there are a number of aspects which can be extended and elaborated, but in a manner consistent both with the phenomena of advertising and the precepts of Austrian methodology.

A feature of the Chamberlinian conception of advertising is that for the advertiser the product precedes the message, whilst for the consumer this is reversed. The analytical convenience of this assumption, however, is at the expense of a realistic understanding of the intracacies of the relationship between product and advertising, as defined in terms of human perception and time. On the producer side, the conception and development of a product cannot be entirely detached from some recognition of the perception of prospective customers; indeed, in extreme cases the product might arise primarily from a communication idea and be designed with this specifically in mind. More generally, the effect of feedback of information on consumer perceptions and their behaviour can lead to joint variation of product characteristics and communications. Over a period of time where there are such changes, even when these are restricted to the content of advertising alone, there is effectively a re-definition of the product. In producer terms, the current projection of his product as a composite of product and advertising features is the relevant definition of product and this subjective view is appropriate whether his advertising is actually reaching the entirety of a target audience or not. For con-sumers, however, the view they take of the product is dependent to some degree on whether they have actually been exposed to advertising and the extent to which their perceptions are influenced. Each consumer, in principle, has his own subjective definition of the composite product which will only coincidentally conform exactly to that of the producer. To maintain the separateness of the product from its advertising is effectively an expression of a belief that advertising has no effect on perceptual and cognitive features and that it is irrelevant whether advertising has been seen or not. Also, in terms of time much advertising, especially that for fast-moving consumer goods, is designed to succeed purchase and consumption of the product; it offers reassurance and the basis of a view about the product to foster the repeat sales on which depends the success of such products.[28]

Another aspect of the relationship between a product and its advertising con-cerns the view taken of information. To consider advertising as information *in toto* (von Mises) or in part (Kirzner) is effectively to separate advertising from the product or products to which it relates. Much depends on the usage of the term 'information', but strictly 'information' is employed either prior or sub-sequent to an actual purchase decision; it is not a complement to the good but a means of formulating or evaluating a decision; it is an input to a decision, not the subject of it. On this basis, because 'cost' is timed at the moment of decision, to separate advertising as information from the purchase decision is to exclude advertising from any category of cost associated with the product; in this sense the price of the product does not apply to the advertising at consumer level (although in setting the price the producer must reflect his advertising outlays). Indeed, such advertising from the recipient's viewpoint is without explicit or imputed price: it is free. The recipient, however, does incur some cost in any response to advertising in terms of the time and effort expended in its recog-nition, but this is not reflected by the product itself or any choice specific to it.

This suggests that an alternative approach is to consider the process of information appraisal *and* the purchase decision as constituting the relevant category of overall choice and to consider the entirety of this process: the 'transaction costs' and the 'purchase decision costs' as a composite. The difficulty here is that the individual components of this composite are them-selves the subject of choice and therefore incur costs. But the timing of these costs in a process is such that they cannot be legitimately aggregated. Indeed, if

this approach is taken — of linking the costs of information search and the pre-
(or post-) decision activity with the final purchase decision, so that the
product's price is in some sense referring to this aggregate — then only if the
product is actually chosen are the appropriate transaction costs reflected in the
outcome. But it is obvious that such a process could culminate in the decision
not to purchase, which leaves the costs of any advertising detached. This
asymmetric treatment of advertising costs is obviated if advertising is treated as
information and not as an entity separate from the product and (as we have
seen above) its price, or some other connection between advertising and the
product is so made to reflect as a composite the cost of the product and its
associated advertising.

The necessary fusion of advertising and product occurs if advertising is
viewed as persuasion. There has been a reluctance amongst economists — even
those basically sympathetic to advertising, such as the Economists Advisory
Group — to view advertising entirely as persuasion. Thus they write:

'As it is generally agreed that no distinction can be made in practice between
information and persuasion contained in any statement, the practical step in
general economic discussion would be to drop the distinction altogether and to
treat all advertising as some kind of information.'[29]

Their election of 'information' rather than 'persuasion' is interesting but fully
consistent with their belief that the general acceptance of a distinction between
information and persuasion is:

'a fundamental misconception, and from the point of view of economic
enquiry, the sooner it is discarded the better'.[30]

Hereafter we presume that advertising is persuasion.

The term 'persuasion' connotes a range of meanings from gentle assistance
when undecided to something barely short of compulsion. Persuasion as a
process may be beneficial or harmful, although the individual's view of it may
be different and indeed change in anticipation of or during the experience or in
retrospect. If persuasion is treated as a 'service' it may be either a 'good' or a
'bad'. It is necessary to distinguish the role of persuasion *per se* from the manner
in which the persuasion is conducted. It is reasonable to conceive of situations
where it is not the fact that persuasion is underway or intended which causes
disutility, but the form the persuasion — the advertising itself — adopts. A
producer's attempt at 'gentle persuasion' may be perceived as 'tasteless' and
'insulting'; although the advertisement may itself be a source of considerable
satisfaction (aesthetic appeal, humour or whatever), the recipient may resent
being persuaded in this 'insidious' manner. What is suggested, therefore, is not
that the product is an occasional composite of inherent product features and
information, as Kirzner suggests, but that in the presence of advertising the
composite is comprised of the inherent product features, the mode of
persuasion and persuasion *per se*.

The role of advertising for the producer *is* persuasion and in this he seeks to be successful. His perception — perhaps enlightened by knowledge acquired by experience or research — of the likely response of consumers to persuasion and the mode of persuasion he employs may lead to innumerable different manifestations of advertising as he seeks to discover whether persuasion is a good and what forms are acceptable. For instance, where persuasion is not favoured, the (persuasive) presentation of more information might be expected, as perhaps with consumer durables. In contrast to this, the 'glamorous' persuasion of cosmetics advertisements seeks to provide excuses rather than reasons for self-indulgence, self-enhancement (or whatever), and the utility of the persuasion is greater perhaps than the objective changes acquired with the product itself. If the consumer is persuaded, that is, accepts persuasion, then the intangibles of the product and its advertising are indeed a composite whole. The coalescence of advertising and the product which occurs when advertising is persuasion, circumvents the problem that arises when advertising as information is separate from the product, of advertising's exclusion from the category of 'cost'. With advertising inherently part of a composite good, the consumer either rejects the composite for a more-favoured alternative or he accepts it and forgoes some other opportunity.

In short, the undoubted informational component of advertising, which is exhibited in various degrees ranging from a statement of product existence to more detailed forms, is entirely separable from the product to which it refers and accordingly detached from the product price. Such information is equivalent to any other form of non-advertised information and specifically does not constitute a component of cost even when a purchase decision occurs. The consumer's choice of information and the selection, evaluation and general consideration of advertised information is separate from the purchase decision itself and hence from its cost. Also there is no relationship between the advertiser's outlays in information transmission and consumers' costs on purchasing. Advertising, however, is intended to be persuasive and its relay of information *is* for this purpose; persuasion is manifestly effective at the act of purchase: any prevarication, etc. is finally overcome at the time of purchase. At this instant the cost is incurred and that 'cost' is the alternative displaced by the acceptance of the price for the composite of product and any persuasion. If advertising has not been seen, or is not thought to have been seen, then the product price paid by such an individual reflects at least his valuation of the product and any advertising outlay reflected in this price is irrelevant to him. For those who are conscious of advertising, the payment of the price is an acceptance (however reluctantly) of the net benefits of the product and its advertising.

3.4 Persuasion and welfare

In terms of the conventional classifications in economics, the topic of persuasion should be incorporated in the theory of consumer behaviour. The dominant theory, however, has no place for persuasion either as a phenomenon or as a possibility. Indeed, the strict neo-classical theory has a place for neither information nor persuasion for the simple but comprehensive reason that preferences are assumed to be known and to reflect a particular set of 'tastes'. Indeed, economics as a discipline regards such matters as the formulation, acquisition or assessment of tastes as outside its sphere of interest and competence. Nevertheless, the analytic convenience of assuming the fixity of taste has been extended to assume that an existing level of tastes is the natural or unadulterated level. However, as Hayek pointed out, to claim any superiority for prior tastes is a denial of cultural evolution, for man is continually learning.[31] In any event, the view is prevalent that any advertising-induced change of tastes is somehow unnatural and not (necessarily) in the consumer's own interest.

This assumption about prior tastes in conjunction with the conventional distinction between production and selling costs, and perfect and imperfect competition, leads to the belief that advertising expense is an unnecessary and wasteful addition to the minimum costs necessary to keep the good in existence. It is thus variously held that advertising is both a symptom and a cause of imperfectly competitive forms which perpetuate allocative deficiencies. Welfare economics, based on assumptions of general equilibrium, zero transaction costs, perfect information and fixed tastes has nevertheless been employed in the assessment of advertising. It should be recognised, however, that the idea that persuasion can be a good or that the disutility of persuasion can be compensated by the *form* of persuasion (as above), is incompatible with these assumptions.

It is a central theme of Kirzner's[32] exposition and delineation of the entrepreneurial role in the market process to show the deficiencies of the static and certain prevailing conceptions of consumer behaviour. Kirzner considers that Robbins's[33] classic account of the nature of the 'economic problem' that confronts consumers in allocating scarce means among competing ends, is incomplete. In the Robbinsian conception, where all necessary information is given and the 'problem' has already been defined, the solution for the consumer is obtainable mechanistically. But when the 'problem' is not pre-set and information is lacking, the features of information search and the learning of tastes and preferences over a period of time become dimensions of problem definition. Under these conditions, advertising's traditional role in changing tastes could be beneficial, but the difficulty or impossibility of comparing tastes frustrates more definitive statements. There are, however, claims to circumvent the problem raised by differing tastes. Thus Stigler and Becker suggest the use of a household production function — analogous to a firm's production function — to create a composite product from an amalgam of product attributes and advertised messages irrespective of tastes. They state:

'We shall argue that it is neither necessary nor useful to attribute to advertising the function of changing tastes . . . The output of a particular firm and its advertising are inputs into a commodity produced and consumed by house-holds.'[34]

This approach is broadly similar to considering advertising features as characteristics of goods.[35] Of similar vintage is the claim by Dixit and Norman[36] to show the extent of excessive advertising, even when evaluation is carried out on the basis of post-advertising tastes which, if justified, rehabilitates neo-classical welfare economics and the empirical methods derived from it, methods which have, nevertheless, been sporadically employed. In particular, the use of demand and cost analysis to establish the (triangular) welfare loss due to higher prices and restricted output attributed to monopoly.[37]

A recent attempt to measure the welfare triangular loss due to monopoly forces) exemplifying the neo-classical view of advertising of Cowling and Mueller[38]), is considered here because it has also been the subject of an Austrian-style critique by Littlechild.[39] In Cowling and Mueller's study, referring to the wastes of combative monopolistic competition they propose:

'Three adjustments to the usual welfare triangle measures of monopoly welfare loss are made to account for the additional expenditures to redistribute monopoly rents, monopoly power induces. First, advertising is added to monopoly profit in calculating the welfare triangle loss to allow for the under-statement of monopoly profit, expenditures of this type produce. Second, all of advertising is added to the welfare loss. This takes the extreme view of advertising as merely an instrument for securing market power. To the extent advertising provides useful information to consumers, this measure overstates the cost of monopoly. Thirdly, all of measured, after tax profits above the competitive cost of capital are used as the estimate of the expenditure incurred by others to obtain control of these monopoly rents.'[40]

Because advertising contributes to higher prices directly and causes 'competitive' reaction in order to gain the monopoly profits available, advertising is a net waste to the extent of one-and-a-half times the expenditure incurred. This result follows Cowling and Mueller's derivation that the conventional welfare loss is approximately one-half monopoly profit, with the two adjustments itemised above.

Providing an alternative view, Littlechild argues that monopoly profit is a social gain. Furthermore, the creation of the product provides consumer surplus on whichever price and quantity combination is offered, so the resultant welfare loss triangle between the monopoly price and the ('subsequent') competitive price is an early realisation of a further gain to consumers' surplus. The role of advertising is to contribute to both the existence of demand by getting the consumer to know of the product opportunity and, in respect of entrepreneurship, in product creation. In a calculation where monopoly profit is re-classified as social gain, the reduction in this profit by the subtraction of advertising outlays underestimates the total gain to that extent. Accordingly, advertising expenditures should be added to 'monopoly' profits to record the net gain.

Several points of our previous discussion are relevant to an understanding of the diametrically-opposed treatments as represented by Cowling and Mueller on the one hand, and Littlechild on the other. A graphical analysis — which both employ — must rest on the Chamberlinian assumption of a given product with advertising as an adjunct; thereby, advertising is strictly informative since, as we have seen, persuasion and the good itself must be considered jointly as a composite product. If the advertising is more than 'bleakly informative', however, the perceptual processes of consumers must be considered and the ensuing heterogeneity of the 'product' definition is inimical to an aggregate analysis, because then the product from the point of view of each consumer is unique, is not objectively known and cannot be represented by a single demand curve. Under these conditions, it follows that the welfare triangle is not defined. Furthermore, the subjectively determined costs incurred by advertisers which translate into advertising outlays measurable in money are not, as data, identifiable as costs to consumers and should play no part in a consumer valuation process unless there is general equilibrium.

In the absence of equilibrium there is a disparity between the producers' outlays for advertising and the valuations of consumers. The producer, in making the decision whether to advertise and to what degree, necessarily forgoes an alternative and so establishes his cost. The determination of cost for any individual consumer is less straightforward; for him it matters crucially whether the advertisement is seen or not, what his perception of its content is, the degree to which he is persuaded, his view on whether persuasion is a good or a bad, and the effect this has in relation to the product advertised. Whatever his perception, he may only act to accept or reject the composite product as he 'sees' it. His specific valuation of the advertising component remains obscure. This is true even in the case of a range of advertised and unadvertised substitutes (or lightly and heavily advertised brands) — for instance, manufacturers' advertised brands and retailers' own brands — where it has been thought that the consumer's valuation of advertising is reflected in any price differential that may obtain.[41] There are several difficulties with this objective approach: if advertising is persuasive, it is inherent in the composite good to a degree which is only knowable (if at all) to an individual and in such a manner that the objective attribution of 'substitutability' is invalidated; of course, there needs to be perfect substitutability for the price differential to be related exclusively to advertising. Moreover, the objective price difference remains the same whether any advertising is seen or not and irrespective of variety in the individual's responses to particular advertisements.

An objective measure of the value of advertising remains elusive too in the contrasting case where advertising is pure information, devoid of persuasion and separate from the product. Undoubtedly, information may have a value but this is specific to an individual in a particular context at a particular time. Consider the case where an advertisement informs of a lower price of a good. Is the value of information the objective difference between the two prices? For an individual who had made a decision to buy and acted on this information it may be, but the same objective difference exists when the advertisement is only seen after purchase, when it is not seen at all or when no purchase occurs. The value is likely to be different in each of these events and the objective difference, which is constant, is only coincidentally an appropriate measure.

It is a necessary consequence of the subjective nature of the value of advertising to each individual producer and each individual consumer, that an 'aggregate value' is unobtainable and even if it were, it would apply only transiently. Although little specifically may be said about the value of aggregate advertising in either a quantitative or qualitative sense, the case could be conceived where there is a mismatch of the producer's perception of the value of advertising and the benefit derived by recipients. Indeed, this is generally the result thought to obtain on the basis of neo-classical analysis. In this case both the Austrians and the neo-classicals stress the role of competition but for quite different reasons. For the Austrians, any excess of advertising would be due to entrepreneurial mistake, a zest to compete or an unexpected but adjustable consequence. In the neo-classical view, the excess is seen as an outcome of imperfectly competitive structures where supra-normal profit or inefficiency obtains. Furthermore, advertising both contributes to and tends to perpetuate this situation because of its role as a 'barrier to entry'.

3.5 Advertising as a barrier to entry

In contrast to the Austrian view, conventional theory posits a state of imperfect competition and considers how this may be maintained. Advertising contributes to this, it is argued, in several ways: by sustaining brand or product loyalty, fostering inertia, or creating some pecuniary disadvantage to entrants through the carry-over of prior advertising or through the reduced charges that large advertisers command and which gives them economies of scale.[42] It is a feature of the Austrian view that in a process of competition there will necessarily be some firms who enjoy an advantage, (reflected by profits), and they will attempt to maintain any superiority by whatever means they can find to offer consumers better value, for in the absence of the ownership of unique and vital resources or governmental licence there is no monopoly.[43] If there is a sole producer, he either awaits competition or presides over an insufficiently attractive enterprise. Otherwise, producers are vulnerable to competitive incursion by a wide variety of means from many different sources and not just from within an 'industry' or variants of the 'product'.

In part, the difference between the state and the process views depends on the role of time. In the process view an existing 'monopoly' position is seen as the reward for competitive success and the culmination of a whole series of risk-laden steps which could have led to exit from the industry, as exemplified by the demise of some unsuccessful competitors. Thus, taking a life-cycle view of the enterprise, the focus on a particular stage (monopoly) requires consideration of adjacent stages to give perspective.

In the process view, the idea of investing in the defence and consolidation of a hard-won market position is a natural property of competition. Furthermore, just by its existence, the enterprise as a whole presents a barrier to a new entrant. But the entrant's disadvantage — and thus the deterrent — arises because the outcome of entry is unforeseeable and *all* the capital required to establish a market position is venture capital. To designate advertising expenditure amongst all other expenditures specifically as a barrier is arbitrary. What is there about advertising expenditure that distinguishes it fundamentally from other inputs, from personnel, access to funds, production expertise or whatever defines a firm's competitive ability? The conventional treatment of advertising as a barrier to entry, however, does isolate advertising in this arbitrary fashion and the impulsion for this is the theory of imperfect competition, with its assumption of the distinction between production and selling costs and its conception of the product. Several aspects and implications of this view deserve further consideration.

The product is assumed to be given and advertising is a subsequent embellishment which differentiates the product in consumers' perceptions. But whilst the advertising confers a separate identity on a brand, sufficient similarity is posited of product form, function, price, advertising and other production costs for alternative organisational forms (either 'more perfectly' competitive or perhaps a regulated monopoly) producing the product to be possible, and indeed, desirable. Thus there is an implicit belief in an objective product and advertising merely persuades consumers that there are differences between brands, with the consequence that the product's price is raised and inefficient forms of production are maintained. In the absence of advertising, either more producers could offer the homogeneous product, or more concentrated methods with lower prices based on production economics would satisfy a greater demand. Secondly, the concept of brand loyalty and its associated features of habit and inertia are largely established in the literature merely by assertion. It is obvious, however, that repetitive behaviour or habit is not confined only to purchase behaviour nor to the set of advertised goods. To establish the role of advertising as a barrier requires the elimination or the isolation of the residual effects of habit and an explanation of how loyalty is then due to advertising rather than to satisfaction with (separate) product features.

A third difficulty of the conventional case is that it remains unclear whether advertising *creates* loyalty or is merely a *response* to habit-prone behaviour. If advertising could create loyalty then its deployment for this purpose would be deliberate and foresighted. Cumulative advertising funds would establish 'goodwill' which would generate funds comparable with the returns from any other investment. To create loyalty, particular qualitative themes would be employed and the size and allocation of advertising funds would reflect this strategy. On the other hand, if advertising was not presumed to create loyalty but was conducted for other pragmatic reasons, then the accumulation of advertising expenses could not necessarily be classified as goodwill because the qualitative content of advertising would not contribute to the loyalty objective.

Economists typically do not consider the qualitative content of advertising; it is treated homogeneously in expenditure terms only. Thus, not only is it presumed that loyalty may be created but the degree of loyalty (the goodwill), depends only on the sum spent on advertising. Such presumptions are little short of heroic, however, because economics has not concerned itself with the mechanisms — communication or otherwise — of how advertising works, its theory does not describe habitual behaviour except as separate decisions which coincidentally have identical outcomes, nor is its theory based on the detailed findings of empirical consumer research. The assertion about loyalty and the assumption of a mechanistic effect of advertising expenditure on behaviour impose a totally unrealistic determinism on the subject of advertising and consumer behaviour, and attributes to advertisers ambitions and objectives which are impossible to achieve.

When an advertiser is unsure of the factors which prompt the selection of his product from a differentiated product class, it must be a speculative decision to incur (heavy) advertising costs exclusively as a barrier. In an oligopoly situation it is not obvious why he, as opposed to some other producer, should venture to exclude a new entrant, whilst the assumption that there is a collective industry response based, perhaps, on tacit collusion is difficult to relate to other aspects of behaviour in oligopoly. Indeed, the collusion which prevents 'price wars' and maintains prices in excess of production costs is frequently thought to be one cause of 'advertising wars'. The speculative use of advertising as a barrier must also be seen in the context of the alternative barriers which the producer could deploy. Advertising is subject to 'wearout' and obsolescence,[44] and its effects are conditional on the capricious behaviour of multitudinous consumers, characteristics which commend alternative strategems which are less uncertain, more direct and durable. Such possibilities arise with negotiated deals with key distributors or through active product and pricing policy.

A further problem with the deliberate utilisation of advertising as a barrier to entry is that it is not necessarily obvious precisely what is to be defended. Markets are not homogeneous: in practice, a variety of different distribution intermediaries and contractual arrangements partition a market. Furthermore, the market is typically segmented with different producers specialising in various ways. In such situations, the attempt to erect barriers channels competition into alternative but related markets. Moreover, with the compartmentalisation of the market, advertising media may not remain a cost-effective means of communication. Although advertising at a conspicuous loss — presumably in the interest of deterring entrants — is a common finding in empirical research, there is considerable doubt about the validity of this work (see Chapter 5). But the scope for loss-making activity is constrained by the apparently inexorable tendency for products to have shorter lives. The attempted creation of such a barrier, loss-making in the short term to ensure an advantage in the longer term, if it proves to be ineffective actually could invite competitive entry. The entrant, by deploying more cost-effective advertising (or some other means), can secure an advantage which the better management of advertising expenditure would deny because loss-making activity makes a firm more vulnerable.

In addition to the above grounds for doubting the validity of the assertion that advertising-induced loyalty is a barrier, it is necessary to consider whether the precise notion of 'loyalty' is justified. Researchers, mainly outside economics, show this to be a more complicated concept than its invocation in connection with barriers suggests.[45] First, there is considerable difficulty in defining 'loyalty'. Is the term to be used for the outcome of a purchase decision or does it describe an input to that decision? Is loyalty the consistent purchasing of a brand, whilst an effort and intention to buy it which for some reason fails is disloyalty? Can there be loyalty to two competing brands? Can loyalty be sustained by advertising alone? Attempts to find the reasons for loyalty have succeeded only in identifying myriad variables relating to all aspects and phases of consumer behaviour and to consumers themselves. The degree to which this information may be utilised by advertisers is still problematical, however. In the frequently-bought product classes in which media display advertising is most conspicuous, both existing producers and prospective entrants must be aware that the low monetary outlay and often negligible perceived risk in switching between brands, give the consumer both considerable expertise in product comparison and account for his susceptibility to 'new' differentiations on an experimental basis. This expertise need not parallel any objective or scientific procedure in product comparison.[46] All that is necessary for consistent purchasing is his belief that he knows which is best; subjective evaluation is sufficient. As a consequence of this, the advertiser is largely impotent in inducing permanent brand change purely by advertising. Indeed, advertising in these situations is mainly to encourage repeat purchase by reassurance and reinforcement.[47]

The effectiveness of the barrier thus posed depends on the perception of the barrier and assessment of the forces to overcome it. Both these aspects are raised when the penetration of a market by a new entrant is considered. Only under certain circumstances will a new entrant to a product class have to match existing advertising to establish credibility with consumers or the co-operation of intermediaries. In other cases, a selective approach in segments reduces the scale of advertising expense. Likewise, the absolute size of the barrier is reduced if greater efficiency or impact of communication is possible. The barrier posed by existing advertising may be lower on qualitative grounds than a quantitative expense suggests. A prospective entrant can employ the existing composites for comparative purposes and gain cost-effective persuasion at their expense, because the initial information about the product's role and purpose has already been conveyed. Also, he has novelty and innovation to pitch against established reputation. To the extent that his product offers perceivable bene-fits, the fundamental task of initial advertising in creating product awareness and trial may be obviated.

Of course, part of the barrier posed by existing advertising is its signal of post-entry advertising capability, which must be seen in conjunction with a response containing new differentiations. Thus, the initial penetration and repeat sales secured or forecast by an entrant may be vulnerable to competitive reaction. The requirement to fund not only initial advertising but subsequent advertising as well as product modification on a continual basis, is the nature of the barrier. But it is important to recognise that it is not the absolute size of this financing which is the barrier, rather the uncertainty of its effects. If expenditure on advertising led to precise and predictable outcomes, there would be no difficulty in justifying and acquiring funds. But its speculative nature and intangible effects are analogous to many other inputs in the productive processes that define competition at any one time. Advertising with other capital requirements acts to deter some competitors who have neither the size, rating, capability or inclination to enter, but it cannot and does not deter all. Indeed, it is precisely advertising's ability to act as a *means* of entry which demonstrates the partiality of the entire barriers argument.

Thus where it is claimed that 'differentiated products' may be sustained by advertising themes, then just as surely can products be created by them, though one cannot attribute creation exclusively to advertising since it is part of a composite. Whereas inertia can cause difficulties to a potential replacement, so too can boring familiarity raise susceptibility to novelty and change. Where prices can be high in a cartel or collusive oligopoly, advertised price reductions or more favourable product features can cause transformation, as for example with air traffic de-regulation.

It may be concluded that the focus on advertising as a barrier to entry has over-emphasised the defensive role that advertising may play. Competition, however, involves both defence and attack and attention to only one aspect ultimately impedes understanding. Advertising can impede entry like any other resource input, but the barrier can be scaled, circumvented or undermined and the evolution of the competitive system creates opportunities for entry for both the large and the small.

3.6 Conclusions

The Austrian economics treatment of advertising centres round a series of insights, none of which is entirely unique to the Austrians, but which as a unified whole does lead to a substantially different conception of the role and significance of advertising in the economy. In the writings of the Austrians the unifying theme has been to link advertising as a means of communication (in its widest sense to include information of existence), to the essential requirements of knowledge for market co-ordination and continuity. Advertising has an important though varying role in the process of competition, conceivably for any participant, since it is not confined merely to those who are already established perhaps with a dominant position but can be the means for a fledgling firm to usurp an existing hold in the market. Clearly, if the origins of an advertising campaign are the reference point, there is no certainty at that time that the particular set of messages employed will create a temporary monopoly position; this might be the perennial hope of advertisers, but the occasions when this does happen are relatively rare and the benefits only transient. If the use of advertising messages alone creates a temporary monopoly then this in itself, though evidence of entrepreneurial alertness, is not to be denigrated as a source (or symptom) of long-term monopoly. Advertising resources are available to others and provide infinite scope to displace an apparently entrenched position.

The Austrian elucidation of the process of competition provides a more realistic integration of market states at different times than do the more stylised analyses emanating from neo-classical economists, where an appropriate static conception is the model typically used. The process view places less emphasis on the achievement of equilibria; there may well be equilibrating tendencies but the inadequacies of information, changing perceptions and the evolving contexts of human action impede both the achieving and the sustaining of equilibria. Of course, the significance of the process view lies in the coherent alternative it offers to the previously dominant model of perfect competition, whose appeal has been out of all proportion to its ability to offer even an approximation to perceived market characteristics. The longevity of this model derives precisely because, as a model, it is not subject to any other test than its own logical completeness and its central place in microeconomics. But, whatever its attractions for theorists, its value in the analysis of phenomena must be subject to other criteria in addition to its own internal logic. Nevertheless, the model has been profoundly influential in the empirical investigation of advertising, though necessarily this has been an indirect influence as any compromise with theory must be. Thus the perfectly competitive model deals with informed participants, prices and homogeneous products within defined industries, even though it is incontestable that, at best, these are only rudimentary simplifications and in certain cases simplification verges on absurdity. The analytical conveniences, which merge into conventions, of taking the product as separate from its advertising and assuming that the objective product is ubiquitously perceived as such, lead to a whole approach which is at variance with the characteristics of advertising. It is inevitable that such enquiry should lead to indeterminate and meaningless results.

The Austrians, characteristically, do not require empirical proofs and therefore they eschew the organisation of the subject to provide testable propositions. This in turn leads to the avoidance of their methodology by the majority of the economics profession, which is dominated by nominal logical positivists. Thus Chiplin and Sturgess[48] write of the Austrian view:

'This view of the market economy does not conveniently lend itself to the development of analytical models or to empirical testing; it relies more on the adherent's "faith" in the accuracy of a particular world view. If the normative analysis of the Austrian school is accepted by the reader, then within this framework of "disequilibrium economics" there would seem to be little point in testing the effects of advertising on economic performance. Advertising is simply one of the instruments by which a market economy adjusts to change. Some deterministic theoretical framework is needed in order to assess the economic effects of advertising and although the disequilibrium approach outlined above allows a discussion of the 'rich detail' of business behaviour, it lends itself to few testable predictions.'

If the purpose of proofs and hypothesis testing is to come to some beliefs, then given the strictly limited domain in which such proofs and tests can be conducted, their contribution to conviction and belief cannot be conclusive; although these may be contributory, along with other forms of information, to the development of a view, they cannot be the sole basis of a view. The contributions to knowledge of the hundreds of empirical papers on advertising and its effects within this dominant tradition have been miniscule and, paradoxically, despite inconsistent and inconclusive results, have nevertheless provided the basis for sectional beliefs.

The Austrian conception of advertising, which is not dogmatic in its predictions, is fully consistent with any number of different outcomes in the workings of a process of competition. This is not, as some might suspect, to have no conception at all; rather it reflects the accumulating evidence of a variety of advertising effects and is consistent with their theoretical development of an entrepreneurial competitive process. In some other respects the Austrian position is less consistent or well founded. It is the case that the process view is derived from analysis of purposeful human action and, in consequence, equilibria are therefore not to be expected as the outcome of a continuously rivalrous process; however, the Austrian analysis of advertising has not rigorously maintained a subjectivist and methodologically individualistic approach.

The treatment of advertising as information and thus in some cases as separate from the product, the perpetuation of the distinction between information and persuasion, and the acceptance of aggregate analyses of advertising, all contravene either the principle of subjectivism or methodological individualism. As a consequence of this, the current Austrian position on the analysis of advertising is not conspicuously distinct nor sharply drawn.

In an elaboration of the Austrian perspective, this chapter has considered the implication of treating all advertising entirely as persuasion. This necessitates that the product be viewed as a (Chamberlinian) composite and then advertising is not separable. For the producer, this means that advertising is just like any other input in the process of production, whilst for the consumer whether, and to what degree, he 'sees' advertising will orientate his perception towards a subjectively defined product. His acceptance or rejection of a composite in a purchase decision involves the valuation of advertising, which can contribute utility or disutility depending on the consumers' view of persuasion and the form it takes. As a consequence of the subjectivist approach, the monetary outlays on advertising cannot be taken as measures of the value of advertising; this is the case whether individual campaign or aggregate advertising statistics are considered and applies also to advertiser, consumer and society at large.

Valuation is necessarily subjective and thereby specific to a particular person, time and situation; nevertheless, some indication of value is derivable from observed action. The existence of advertising, its ubiquity, divisibility, diversity and its competitive structure are generally indicators of its efficacy both to its employers and others, and of course it is this use which sustains the process and determines the competitive outcomes.

References

1. Kirzner, I. M., 'The "Austrian" Perspective on the Crisis', in Bell, D. and Kristol, I. (eds.), *The Crisis in Economic Theory*, New York: Basil Books, 1981, pp.111–122.
2. Littlechild, S. C., *The Fallacy of the Mixed Economy*, Institute of Economic Affairs, Hobart Paper 80, 1978.
3. Kirzner, I. M., 'On the Method of Austrian Economics', in Dolan, E. G. (ed.), *The Foundations of Modern Austrian Economics*, Kansas City: Sheed and Ward, 1976, p.40.
4. *Ibid.*, p.43.
5. Buchanan, J. M., *Cost and Choice*, Chicago: Markham Publishing Co., 1969.

6. Vaughn, K. I., 'Does it Matter that Costs are Subjective?', *Southern Economic Journal*, vol. 46, 3, Jan. 1980, pp.702–715.
7. *Ibid.*, p.710.
8. Hayek, F. A., *The Counter-Revolution of Science: Studies on the Abuse of Reason*, Glencoe, Illinois: Free Press, 1955, p.39.
9. Lachmann, L. M., 'On the Central Concept of Austrian Economics: Market Process', in Dolan, E. G. (ed.), *op cit.*, p.128.
10. Kirzner, I. M., *Competition and Entrepreneurship*, Chicago: The University of Chicago Press, 1973, p.35.
11. Mises, L. von, *Human Action*, 3rd revised edition, Chicago: Henry Regnery Company, 1966, p.97.
12. *Ibid.*, p.290.
13. Kirzner, I. M., 1973, *op cit.*, p.48.
14. Lachmann, L. M., 1976, *op cit.*, p.128.
15. Mises, L. von, *op cit.*, p.249.
16. *Ibid.*, p.320.
17. *Ibid.*, p.320.
18. *Ibid.*, p.323.
19. *Ibid.*, p.320.
20. *Ibid.*, p.322.
21. Kirzner, I. M., 1973, *op cit.*, but see also Kirzner, 'Advertising', *The Freeman*, Sept. 1972.
22. Chamberlin, E. H., *The Theory of Monopolistic Competition*, 8th edition, Cambridge, Mass.: Harvard University Press, 1962, p.280.
23. Kirzner, I. M., 1973, *op cit.*, p. 155.
24. *Ibid.*, p.159.
25. *Ibid.*, p.156.
26. *Ibid.*, p.163.
27. *Ibid.*, p.179.
28. Ehrenberg, A. S. C., 'Repetitive Advertising and the Consumer', *Journal of Advertising Research*, April 1974, pp.25–33.
29. Economists' Advisory Group, *The Economics of Advertising*, Advertising Association, London, 1967, pp.74.
30. *Ibid.*, p. 75.
31. Hayek, F. A., 'The Non-Sequitur of the Dependence Effect', *Southern Economic Journal*, 27, April 1961, pp.346–48.
32. Kirzner, I. M., 1973, *op cit.*, chs. 2, 3.
33. Robbins, L., *An Essay on the Nature and Significance of Economics Science*, 2nd edn., London: Macmillan and Co., 1935.
34. Stigler, G. J. and Becker, G., 'De Gustibus non est Disputandum', *American Economic Review*, vol. 67, no. 2, March 1977, p.84.
35. Rosen, S., 'Advertising, Information and Product Differentiation', in Tuerck, D. G. (ed.), *Issues in Advertising: The Economics of Persuasion*, Washington, D.C.: American Enterprise Institute for Public Policy Research, 1978, pp.161–191.
36. Dixit, A. and Norman, V., 'Advertising and Welfare', *The Bell Journal of Economics*, vol. 9, no. 1, 1978, pp.1–17.

37. See, for instance, Needham, D., *The Economics of Industrial Structure, Conduct and Performance*, New York: Holt, Rinehart and Winston, 1978, p. 240.
38. Cowling, K. and Mueller, D. C., 'The Social Costs of Monopoly Power', *Economic Journal*, vol. 55, December 1978, pp.727–48.
39. Littlechild, S. C., 'Misleading Calculations of the Social Costs of Monopoly Power', *The Economic Journal*, 91, June 1981, pp.348–363.
40. Cowling, K. and Mueller, D. C., *op cit.*, p.733.
41. Telser, L. G., 'Supply and Demand for Advertising Messages', *American Economic Review*, 56, May 1966, pp.457–66.
42. Comanor, W. S. and Wilson, T. A., 'Advertising, Market Structure and Performance', *Review of Economics and Statistics*, No. 49, 1974, pp.423–40.
43. Kirzner, I. M., 1973, *op cit.*, ch. 3.
44. Corkindale, D. R. and Newall, J., 'Advertising Thresholds and Wearout', *European Journal of Marketing*, vol. 12, no. 5, 1978, pp.329–78.
45. Brown, G. H., 'Brand Loyalty—Fact or Fiction?', *Advertising Age*, vol. 24, 1953.
46. Batsell, R. R. and Wind, Y., 'Product Testing: Current Methods and Needed Developments', *Journal of the Market Research Society*, vol. 22, no. 2, 1980, pp.115–37.
47. Ehrenberg, A. S. C., 1974, *op cit.*
48. Chiplin, B. and Sturgess, B., *Economics of Advertising*, 2nd edition, London: Holt, Rinehart and Winston with the Advertising Association, 1981, pp.101–2.

4

Advertising and consumer behaviour

4.1 Introduction

The dominant motivation for both theoretical and empirical studies of advertising and consumer behaviour has been the need to ascertain the *effectiveness* of persuasive communication in the market place. Historically, this need has been confined to producers and advertisers but, as earlier chapters have demonstrated, it is increasingly necessary that public policymakers subject their views on the nature of advertising effectiveness to greater scrutiny. The requirements sought of advertising and the criteria by which to judge it are different for its producers, recipients and policymakers but, nevertheless, each is dependent to some extent on an understanding of how advertising works and its *effects* on recipients. It is ironic that many advertising agents share with advertising's sternest critics the belief that the main effects of advertising are to change people's minds and, thereby, their behaviour as consumers and, thereafter so to reinforce existing mental predispositions as to ensure that customers are disinclined to deviate from their established pattern of brand preference. Such is the tendency in Western industrial societies to interpret human behaviour in terms of underlying 'psychological causes' that this has also become the commonplace view of advertising with many ramifications.

The approach adopted here is centred on the main competing hypotheses of the mechanism and contexts of advertising; thus advertising is considered in general and there is little specific concern with the composition of individual advertisements or the circumstances and characteristics of individual recipients. Consideration at this higher level of aggregation is warranted if the overwhelming detail of advertising phenomena is to be made comprehensible. Moreover, because advertising is frequently *mass* communication and the advertiser is obliged to consider aggregate rather than individualistic behaviour to manage his advertisements, this level of consumer aggregation is both practically relevant and indeed is the first step to a more disaggregated approach. Likewise, for policy purposes it is necessary to establish a sufficiently general relationship between advertising and behaviour so that any pathological or atypical effects can both be discerned and given perspective.

The appropriate disciplinary base for present purposes derives primarily from social psychology and marketing. Of course, consumer psychology and producers' marketing behaviour with respect to advertising are closely related and in view of the marketing orientation of the next chapter on producer behaviour the emphasis here is towards, but is not confined to, consumer psychology. The strictly limited adoption by economists and other specialists of psychological rationales of advertising effects suggests that the literature has proved difficult to penetrate. Although disciplinary specialisation is both understandable and indeed necessary, the compartmentalisation of knowledge can be an impediment to wider understanding and informed appraisal. Moreover, the prevailing view, as demonstrated below, is itself based on a selective and partial interpretation of the literature. It is a matter of concern that a significant body of knowledge should be so represented and this fully justifies both an elaboration and re-examination of relevant literature. Accordingly, in this chapter the prevailing view of how advertising works is subjected to critical evaluation and an alternative explanation of the effects of advertising on consumers is advanced.

4.2 How advertising works: the prevailing view

Because of the practical difficulties involved in assessing the precise effectiveness of advertising in terms of sales — particularly the problem of unravelling the effects of advertising from the effects of other elements of the marketing mix — the majority of researchers have concentrated their efforts on measuring those effects of advertising which are apparently more amenable to definition and identification and to the treatment of advertising's effects and effectiveness in terms of its unique contribution to the marketing mix, namely, direct commercial communication with consumers. Advertising has been evaluated by means of measuring the effects which it alone has upon consumers — its capacity to create awareness, inform, establish liking for specific brands, and so on — and each of these effects has been measured through the use of standard types of psychological test.

This approach to the measurement of the consequences of advertising is commendable in that it simplifies a complex problem; if the sales effectiveness of advertising cannot be readily isolated and ascertained, it is sensible to measure as far as possible its known definable effects and to set managerial objectives for advertising in terms of these effects: the creation of awareness, for instance. But this pragmatic step has resulted in a formalisation of the advertising process, a theoretical understanding of how advertising operates which is inappropriate both for the majority of corporate advertising decisions and for the creation and assessment of public policy with respect to advertising. The error of this understanding stems from its tendency to describe the psychological effects of advertising as a series of contingent mental states, a sequence of mental effects each of which leads logically to the next and, as long as the process is not aborted, inexorably to purchase behaviour. Thus consumer brand choice is understood as a function of purchase intention, which is a function of preference; preference is a function of liking which is portrayed as a function of awareness. Advertising is a force which not only creates each of the pre-purchase mental states posited, but which is capable of moving sections of the community from one state to another in order to make purchase possible.

The fundamental idea of a sequence of mental events which prefigure behaviour, variously termed the 'hierarchy of effects' and the 'communications spectrum', has been expressed in several ways. One widely-used basis for the setting of advertising objectives and the measurement of advertising effectiveness devised by Colley,[1] conceptualises consumers' responses in terms of five stages — unawareness, awareness, comprehension, conviction and action. Colley makes very clear the underlying connection between consumer behaviour and the psychological stages which are held to prefigure it and upon which his model is based:

This concept is applied common sense. It breaks the subject up into logical and comprehensible steps. It begins with the obvious assumption that advertising is a communication force. Advertising does not physically impel the consumer toward the purchase of goods; its purpose is to create a state of mind conducive to purchase. Advertising, therefore, is one of several communication forces which, acting singly or in combination, move the consumer through successive levels of the "communications spectrum".[2]

An alternative but similar model has been proposed by Lavidge and Steiner;[3] their view of how consumers react to advertising and their approach to the measurement of advertising effectiveness has had considerable impact upon both advertising practice and the academic study of the subject.[4] The sequence depicted by Lavidge and Steiner comprises:

awareness knowledge	}	cognitive responses measured by aided recall, brand awareness surveys, etc.
liking preference	}	effective responses measured by projective tests, rating scales, attitude tests, etc.
conviction purchase	}	conative responses measured by purchase intentions, sales audits, etc.

Advertising is portrayed by these authors as 'a force, which must move people up a series of steps' — the assumed mental levels which are the building blocks of their model. More revealing, they propose that the key functions of advertising research are:

1. The identification of critical pre-purchase steps for particular consumer groups.

2. The calculation of the proportion of each segment who are at each level.
3. The identification of the most significant individuals and groups at each level so that advertising goals and plans may be drawn up in such a way as to guarantee accessibility to them.

Information processing

These hierarchy of effects models of consumers' responses to advertising bear much resemblence to AIDA, the salesman's mnemonic which casts consumer behaviour as a process of attention $\rightarrow$ interest $\rightarrow$ desire $\rightarrow$ action. In the terminology of the social psychologist, each of these models portrays advertising's effect on the consumer as a logical sequence of pre-behavioural mental events, beginning with cognitive (thought-related) activities and proceeding via affective (attitudinal, preferential) states to conative (behavioural) tendencies and thence to behaviour itself. (Behaviour is usually conceived as the purchase of a chosen brand from an evoked set which comprises several competing brands.) All hierarchy of effects models derive, moreover, from the information processing view of human behaviour postulated within the currently predominant 'behaviour science' paradigm — cognitive psychology — which is the foundation of much contemporary thought and action in consumer research and marketing management. Psychological theories of cognitive information processing are generally complex in themselves but rely on several much simpler ideas: the environment gives rise to informational stimuli which are screened, filtered and partly accepted by the individual and transferred via short and (perhaps) long term memories and other intra-personal processes into a behavioural output. The intermediate products of this process are *beliefs* about and *attitudes* towards the stimulus object in question (a product, a behaviour, a person) and an *intention to behave* in a manner which is consistent with these beliefs and attitudes.[5] The behavioural response which is the ultimate output of the process is assumed to be entirely consistent with the behavioural intention. Indeed, this process of intellectualisation — attitude formation/attitude change and intention culminating in a consistent and predictable pattern of overt behaviour — underlies the major theoretical work in marketing research during the last two decades.[6]

The particular view of advertising's effects depicted in this approach is firmly based on the assumption that advertising is a powerful means of engendering consumer responses which are of benefit to producers. Ehrenberg and Goodhardt[7] term this view 'the *strong* theory of advertising' in which:

'Advertising is expected to play a major role. First, it has to create awareness of the product or brand. It then has to turn awareness into interest, and the interest into a real desire or conviction to buy. This culminates in action, i.e. purchase of the item. In such models, persuasive advertising has therefore to convince the customer of the item's worth before he actually buys it. This is a big task.'

It is the assumed ability of advertising to shape interest and build conviction at the *pre-purchase* stage which forms the essence of the strong advertising hypothesis. This approach emphasises advertising at the expense of the other elements of the marketing mix, but its acceptance has implications well beyond the problems of managerial decision-making in marketing. If this hypothesis is correct, public policy with respect to advertising must take fully into consideration the tendency of this form of communication to create and modify consumers' attitudes and intentions as a pre-condition of purchase behaviour. But how valid is the 'strong' advertising hypothesis?

4.3 Consumer decision-making: theory and practice

If the view of advertising as a strong force, capable of changing consumers' minds and, thereby, their behaviours, provides the accurate description of commercial and customer behaviours upon which sound policy may rest, it should be a relatively straightforward matter to demonstrate empirically two broad patterns of consumer choice. First, there should be a definite logical sequence of events — from cognition to affect to conation — through which the potential buyer moves rationally and predictably. Most adoption models employed in marketing view the consumer 'as securing information, processing it, and evaluating it. We assume that he makes his decision in the rational manner of an economic man based on the intrinsic qualities of the information obtained.'[8] The discovery that other sequences are prevalent or that no sequence at all is discernible or that consumer choice tends to be largely unplanned would invalidate the general view of consumers' response to advertising. Secondly, there should be high correlational consistency between purchase behaviour (e.g. brand choice) and psychological factors which are assumed to be its precursors, over a variety of situations and contexts. In particular, measures of attitudes towards a given product should correlate highly and consistently with measures of behaviour towards the same product.

The empirical evidence on consumer choice indicates that the depiction of consumers as rational, problem-solving beings is actually a highly limited description of buyer behaviour. Extended problem solving, Howard[9] argues, occurs relatively infrequently: for example, in situations in which a new brand within an entirely new product class is introduced to the consumer; the vast majority of consumers' purchase choices can actually be far more accurately described as routinised behavioural responses. Robertson[10] argues, moreover, that it is unrealistic to retain the notion of the rational consumer in the face of mounting evidence that many purchases are socially and situationally determined, notably in the case of so-called impulse buying. At least two forms of the adoption process model are therefore required and the applicability of one or the other to any particular purchase situation depends on such factors as the significance of the purchase to the consumer, the extent to which he or she is able to differentiate brands, reference group influences (stemming from the conspicuousness and social significance of the product in question) and the capacity of the consumer to take risks and handle complex decision procedures.[11]

As perusal of such leading periodicals as the *Journal of Consumer Research* and the *Journal of Marketing Research* will confirm, the empirical evidence gathered during the last decade with respect to consumers' use of information, their capacity and/or willingness to undertake rational, comparative evaluations of brand attributes and to judge consistently between brands by means of complex information processing tends to emphasise that effects models have only limited relevance. For instance, an investigation by Jacoby, Chestnut and Silberman[12] of consumers' understanding and use of additional nutrition-related information printed on food product labels (which was, incidentally, undertaken in response to consumerists' calls for the augmentation of such information) led to the conclusion that:

'the vast majority of consumers neither use nor comprehend nutrition information in arriving at food purchase decisions.'[13]

Other researchers[14] have concluded that the provision of additional information to consumers does not result in their making more economically-rational brand choices. The capacity or willingness or need consumers have to search for, process and evaluate information appears to be far smaller than is often expected and predicted. Moreover, there is evidence that they infer erroneous information from such indicators as price.[15]

Critical attention has also been drawn to the differing numbers of stages posited by the separate versions of the hierarchy of effects model. Most versions suggest four, five or six but it has been vigorously argued that only the two extremes, awareness and adoption, are necessary to describe the buying process.[16] Actually, Ehrenberg's portrayal[17] of the process in terms of three stages — awareness, trial and repeat buying (ATR) — is probably more descriptively useful than this and figures in a number of commercial marketing research investigations. The ATR model stresses that consciousness of and interest in an advertised brand rarely lead to immediate adoption (repeated purchase); yet the absence from the model of intervening psychological processes such as attitudes and intentions emphasises that they are not necessary to an understanding of brand choice and repeat buying. At best, awareness leads to trial purchase and use and the evaluation of the selected brand takes place while it is *in use*. Repeat buying is consequent upon the performance of the brand during this trial period and there is no need for the elaborate theorisation about mediating psychological stages or for the analogies with computer systems' data processing facilities which form the content of so much modelling of consumer behaviour in marketing. As will be seen later, this approach suggests a radically different role for advertising from that inherent in models which are based on the information processing idea.

Consumer commitment

The portrayal of consumers' reactions to advertising in terms of an information-processing sequence or an effects hierarchy suggests the cumulative, pre-purchase commitment of the eventual buyer to the advertised brand: as marketing communications move him progressively through the postulated mental states whose end is purchase behaviour, he becomes increasingly *convinced* that this purchase is necessary, increasingly *committed* to the brand in question. Pre-purchase commitment is an essential output of the cognitive → affective → conative progression.

Dissatisfaction with the descriptive validity of this sequence may be traced to the inability of social psychologists and consumer researchers to demonstrate the underlying proposition of their models to the effect that individuals' attitudes (affect) pre-figure and determine their behaviours. Fishbein[18] sums up thus:

'After more than 70 to 75 years of attitude research, there is still little, if any, consistent evidence supporting the hypothesis that knowledge of an individual's attitude toward some object will allow one to predict the way he will behave with respect to that object. Indeed, what little evidence there is to support any relationship between attitude and behaviour comes from studies that a person tends to bring his attitude into line with his behaviour rather than from studies demonstrating that behaviour is a function of attitude.'

This is, of course, precisely the opposite relationship to that inherent in the information processing and 'strong advertising' views; as such it hardly suggests pre-behavioural psychological commitment.

Attempting to come to terms with this problem, Ray[19] has argued that the sequence incorporated in the original hierarchy of effects model is but one of three which describe consumer behaviour under varying conditions (i.e. in different situations). Cognition → affect → conation, the 'learning hierarchy', describes consumers' response to advertising:

'when the audience is *involved* in the topic of the campaign and when there are *clear differences between alternatives,*'

for example, the adoption process involved in the trial and acceptance of radical innovations.[20] In the vast majority of instances of consumer purchasing, however, inter-personal rather than marketer-dominated communications exert the primary influences on consumer choice. As a result of observation and imitation, behaviour may (and Fishbein suggests it usually does) precede affective and cognitive events: so subversive has been the discovery that this often is the case to the expectations of cognitive psychologists that several major explicative frameworks have been created, notably Festinger's dissonance reduction theory[21] and Bem's self-attribution theory.[22] Ray[23] hypothesises that a conative–affective–cognitive response to advertising is probable in situations in which:

'the audience has been involved but the *alternatives have been almost in-distinguishable*. The consumer . . . is forced to make a choice or behaviour on the basis of some *non-media or non-marketing communication source*. Then he or she changes attitude in order to bolster that choice — often on the basis of experience with the chosen alternative. Finally, learning itself occurs on a selective basis, in order to bolster the original choice by response to messages that are supportive of it.'

Festinger's theory predicts that post-purchase advertising stimulates the attitudinal and intellectual changes which justify preceding brand choice even if (perhaps *particularly* if) experience with the brand is negative. Thus, it has been argued, purchasers of motor cars tend to make use of advertisements *after* rather than *before* buying (presumably for reassurance) and the withdrawal of introductory price discount offers leads to dissonance — though even commonplace observation has led to alternative explanations of these phenomena. Although the theory of cognitive dissonance is consistent with the conation → affect → cognition sequence, it continues to attribute considerable power, albeit at a post-purchase stage, to advertising. Bem's self-attribution theory dispenses with internal, psychological processes in order to explain the behaviour → attitude sequence. Bem argues that measures of attitude refer not to some intra-personal, mental event or process but simply to verbal behaviour — the words in which the individual describes his past behaviour. For example, he infers his liking for a specific product or brand ('forms an attitude towards it') as a result of observing his frequent purchase and use of that product or brand.

Bem's theory is also relevant to the third sequence described by Ray, the 'low involvement hierarchy' which comprises cognition → conation → affect. Here, advertising has an initial cognitive effect upon the consumer who is *uninvolved* in its subject; cognitive activity is not sufficient to modify the recipient's attitudes but ensures awareness of the advertised brand's name and image. When an opportunity to purchase the brand arises, the consumer's awareness may stimulate trial. The formation of attitudes is assumed to occur at the post-purchase stage as a result of the consumer's experience with the product, i.e. the outcomes or consequences of having used it. The situations in which this cognitive → conative → affective sequence is likely to occur are described by Ray[24] as those in which:

'there are *minimal differences between alternatives* or when low involve-ment makes actual differences unimportant to the audience.'

From a series of laboratory experiments and simulations, Ray concluded that the low involvement occurs rather more frequently than the learning hierarchy; the dissonance–attribution effect is comparatively rare. Involvement or commitment emerges as the principal explicative variable and low involvement consumer behaviour, which has long been systematically ignored, has recently attracted considerable research attention. The low involvement thesis is, however, further supported by the consistent finding of a rapid rate of decay of consumers' memories of advertising messages. Whether this phenomenon is described in terminology drawn from cognitive or behaviourist psychology, it is clear that most consumers have great difficulty in recalling verbally the advertisements and messages to which they have been exposed.[25]

The importance of low involvement on the part of members of the audiences of televised advertisements is the subject of a seminal paper by Krugman[26] in which he notes that:

'Psychologists have long asserted that the effects of "latent" learning are only or most noticeable at the point of reward.'

In the context of *consumer* behaviour,

'The purchase situation is the catalyst that reassembles or brings out all the potentials for shifts in salience that have accumulated up to that point. The product or package is then suddenly seen in a new, "somehow different" light although nothing verbalisable may have changed *up to that point*. What we ordinarily call "change of attitude" may then occur after some real interval, however minute.'

Nor is this post-behavioural formation of an attitude towards the purchased item the simple rationalisation assumed by dissonance theory: it is the natural response of the individual to his purchase and would be more easily observed if products always provided the consequences expected by consumers.

The idea that consumer behaviour is characterised by low commitment has recently come to the fore. Rejecting the notion that customers generally engage in extensive pre-purchase searches for and evaluation of information, Robertson[27] contends that their commitment to most consumer product brands is so low as to render the opportunity costs demanded by such problem-solving procedures too high to be worthwhile (a point which would explain consumer rejection of additional nutritional information *in situ*). Although repetition of advertisements might eventually stimulate some interest and may catalyse trial purchase as and when an opportunity to buy occurs, the essentially passive consumer does not experience pre-behavioural attitude change or form purchase intentions or, normally, actively seek situations in which purchase would be possible. At best, he acquires the knowledge of the existence of brands on which trial depends. Such trial purchasing is obviously situationally-determined and any pattern of repeat buying which occurs is determined by the use of the product and the consequences thereof. Advertising indeed plays a role — by stimulating exploratory purchase and this may result in temporary or permanent brand switching but hardly by such forceful means as inducing pre-purchase modification of attitudes. Repeat purchase behaviour is primarily a function of the outcome of previous behaviour with the item. Engel and Blackwell[28] have recently stated that the information-processing based model of high involvement consumer behaviour, in whose promulgation they were uniquely instrumental, applies to only a minority of purchases: 'Most items, quite frankly, are not sufficiently important to justify this kind of activity.' Their conclusion is supported by Olshavsky and Granbois:[29]

'A significant proportion of purchases may not be preceded by a decision process. This conclusion does not simply restate the familiar observation that purchase behaviour rapidly becomes habitual, with little or no prepurchase processes occurring after the first few purchases. We conclude [from an extensive literature review] that for many purchases a decision process never occurs, not even on the first purchase.'

The antecedents of consumer behaviour, from which predictions of such outcomes as brand choice may be predicted, are to be found in previous behavioural learning, adherence to social norms, and the shaping influences of social situations. Not all consumer behaviour may occur in the absence of preceding, determinative and researchable psychological processes but most consumer choices take place in the purchase situation itself rather than via antecedent mental deliberations. Significantly, there can also be low consumer involvement with the communicated stimuli *per se* as and when they impinge upon the recipient. Not only might the advertising message be ineffectual as far as initiating complex information processing is concerned: it may well be missed altogether, though the possibility exists that the involvement with an advertisement *per se* can be greater than the involvement with the composite of advertisement and the product to which it relates, but this, of course, has the same behavioural effects.

What, then, is the role of advertising in consumer behaviour? Quite different conclusions from those drawn from information-processing theorisation are required, given the sheer volume of transactions concerning low involvement choices, where even discernible brand differences are unlikely to engender high ego involvement, the risks of product failure are low, and where the economic and social consequences of mistakes are generally minute. Moreover, since the advertisements for the majority of such brands are rarely distinguishable from each other or capable of contributing much to the differentiation of brands either prior to or after purchase, commitment on the part of consumers may actually be reduced. Recognition of this may act as a spur to the creation of more acceptable or memorable copy, though a frequent response is mere repetition of existing advertising. Advertising is frequently sufficiently persuasive to arouse curiosity and given the necessary opportunity stimulates trial, but no amount of persuasive marketing communication can establish and/or maintain loyalty to a brand which does not fulfil in use the expectations consumers have of it. The vast majority of consumer brands are of this kind and the bulk of advertising is concerned with them. The function of such advertising is to defend: to maintain sales as far as possible by reinforcing the customer's positive experience with the advertised brand. Brand usage itself tends to increase commitment to a product class and advertising for the brands within it: behaviour induces cognitive as well as affective responses. Purchase and use alert the customer to product class advertising and although this may not be overtly persuasive (consisting often of no more than the brand's name and packaging), it is, nevertheless, the only cost-effective means available to producers to confirm and reinforce consumer behaviour or to stimulate trial of alternative brands. Contrary to the impression projected by the information-processing based models of consumer choice extant in the marketing literature, the advertising/consumer behaviour relationship is actually quite simple. Indeed, such is the simplicity of the situation described above that only the simplest of consumer behaviour models captures its essence. Ehrenberg and Goodhardt's *'weak* theory of advertising', in which awareness, trial and reinforcement[30] are the salient variables which describe (and possibly explain) consumer behaviour, is based on this understanding of the role of marketer-dominated communication. Even *initial* purchase may result, however, from reference group and other social and situational influences over which the producer has no direct and severely limited indirect control, rather than from advertising. Whatever the source of the influence, it has no power beyond engendering passing interest and, perhaps, cursory comparative evaluation; it is certainly, of itself, incapable of building preference or conviction. Even advertising's ability to elicit brand trial is circumscribed by the individual's experience with other advertisements and similar products as well as by the myriad competing influences which claim his time. If advertising engenders curiosity which happens to elicit trial, its pre-purchase work is done; its role thereafter is primarily to remind the buyer of any benefits provided by the chosen item but its capacity to do this depends crucially on the performance of the brand in question and the judgement made by consumers with respect to the consequences of using it.

4.4 Consumers' attitudes and behaviour

While it is capable of embracing many of the concepts of cognitive psychology which have found a place in the study of consumer behaviour (selective perception and cognitive dissonance, for example), a 'weak theory of advertising' is also fully consistent with an approach to this subject which concentrates exclusively upon behaviour without recourse to explanation in terms of intra-personal mental events and processes which are presented as the pre-behavioural determinants of overt action. 'Awareness' implies the capacity to recognise brands, to discriminate, say between a newly-launched brand and existing members of its product class. The ability so to discriminate is recognisable from behaviour, usually verbal, in which the respondent indicates the capacity to isolate the new item in some way from the existing brands, e.g. by repeating its brand name; it is not possible to discern directly any internal perceptual processes in terms of which this discriminative behaviour is usually described and 'explained' in the consumer behaviour literature. Similarly 'trial' is a behaviour, as is 'repeat buying'. Without denying that psychological events may intervene between trial and adoption, this behaviourist viewpoint stresses the ambiguous and covert nature of such events and focuses instead upon the behavioural consequences of trial and the pattern of repeat purchase and consumption which follows. Behaviour whose consequences result in repetition of that behaviour is said to be reinforced by its consequences. The incidence of desirable consequences in the process of product trial usually results in further purchasing of the brand in question: the buyer's purchase act is positively reinforced by the product. Purchase of a product whose consequences in use are such that it is not re-purchased is negatively reinforced. Whether any given behaviour is repeated depends, therefore, upon the contingencies of reinforcement inherent in the situation in which behaviour occurs rather than upon the supposed mental precursors of and reactions to it. At the very least this behaviourist approach is based upon the claim that the prediction of behaviour is likely to be more accurate if it is based upon knowledge of the individual's reinforcement history rather than his so-called 'psychological' attitudes.[31]

The behaviourist framework of analysis is a far cry from the cognitively-based sequences which have thus far been discussed and its relevance to consumer research has yet to be demonstrated. That relevance can be assessed by giving further consideration to the information-processing theory upon which both the cognition/affect/conation sequences and the 'strong theory of advertising' are founded.

Attitudes, intentions and behaviour

Central to the information-processing paradigm which forms the basis of marketing models of consumer behaviour is the proposition that behaviour approximates behavioural intentions, which are a function of attitudes and beliefs. The search for evidence of the attitudinal-behavioural consistency which ought to underlie the proposed relationship has for decades absorbed the attention of both consumer researchers and social psychologists. But the search has proved fruitless and the evidence which has accrued suggests a re-interpretation of the nature of consumer choice. Although the view that behaviour towards an object would be consistent with the subject's attitude towards that object regardless of situation received some important setbacks much earlier, it was in the late 1960s that overwhelming evidence was marshalled to undermine it. After a thorough review of those studies from which unambiguous conclusions were available, Wicker[32] wrote that:

'Taken as a whole, these studies suggest that it is considerably more likely that attitudes will be unrelated to overt behaviours than that attitudes will be closely related to actions. Product-moment correlation coefficients relating the two kinds of responses are rarely above 0.30, and often are near zero. Only rarely can as much as 10 per cent of the variance in overt behavioural measures be accounted for by attitudinal data. In studies in which data are dichotomised, substantial proportions of subjects show attitude–behaviour discrepancies. This is true even when subjects scoring at the extremes of attitudinal measures are compared on behavioural indices.'

Wicker suggested that correlations might be improved by the inclusion of personal factors (other attitudes; competing motives; verbal, intellectual and social abilities; activity levels) and situational factors (actual or considered presence of other people; normative behavioural prescriptions; the specificity with which the attitude object is defined; unforeseen events; the actual and expected consequences of behaviour with respect to the attitude object) in the prediction of behaviour. With respect to the latter set of variables, he postulated that 'the more similar the situations in which verbal and overt behavioural responses are obtained, the stronger will be the attitude–behaviour relationship', and it is largely as a result of the operationalisation of these hypothesised situational influences that attitude–behaviour research was revolutionised during the 1970s.

This revolution in thought has been largely the result of the work of Fishbein[33] whose 'behavioural intentions model' posits that, under certain specific conditions, behaviour is predictable from measures of behavioural intentions. The latter comprise measures of:

1. The individual respondent's attitude towards an act (e.g. buying or using margarine) and
2. The degree to which the individual is motivated to conform to others' expectations of how he should behave. Very high correlations (typically > 0.8) of behavioural intentions and behaviour have been obtained under the closely prescribed conditions specified and within the limitations of the model's definitions.

The Fishbein intentions model is concerned with *attitudes towards specified actions involving an object* rather than with the much wider *attitude towards the object* from which so many other researchers have attempted to predict precise behaviours. Thus, rather than attempting to forecast purchase of a particular brand from responses to very general attitude statements concerning its product class, it is necessary to obtain both behavioural and attitudinal measures of a highly specific behaviour towards the object, e.g. the purchase of Brand A from a local supermarket as part of a regular shopping trip. Further, the model does not rely solely upon attitudes towards the act in order to ascertain behavioural intentions; it also takes many aspects of the (social) situation into account as well as the individual's reinforcement history. The resulting behavioural intentions are moreover predictive of behaviour only when that behaviour follows immediately upon the expression of the intentions. The longer the temporal interval separating them, the greater is the possibility of extraneous situational intervention and that behaviour will fail to approximate closely to the expressed intention. Some spheres of human activity are, of course, marked by a low incidence of situational intervention, especially where there has been an expression of real commitment or where there are social pressures to conform. Whilst such features are on occasions applicable even to the routine purchase of fast-moving consumer goods — and some advertising platforms attempt to create such a situation — the artic- ulation of an intention is rarely significant in itself and deviation from it has minimal consequences. Indeed, the unreliability of stated intentions — even when expressed in probabilistic terms is a contributory factor to the high failure rate of new consumer products — even for the purchase of higher-commitment consumer durables.

From their analysis of 142 studies of attitudinal–behavioural relationships Ajzen and Fishbein[34] conclude that relatively high correlations ($r \geqslant 0.40$) are obtained only when the measures of attitude and behaviour correspond closely in terms of the target towards which the action is directed and the precise action itself; full correspondence requires, in addition, that these measures match in terms of the context in which the action occurs and its timing. When corres- pondence is low, attitudinal–behavioural correlation tends to be low ($r < 0.40$) and/or statistically insignificant.

The fact that attitudinal–behavioural consistency is high only when the attitudes or intentions involved are those which immediately precede the behaviour in question and refer to it in such precise terms of correspondence is of great significance in the context of advertising and consumer behaviour because it indicates quite clearly that situational interventions (whether related to the issue, e.g. other advertising or factors extraneous to it, a quarrel or what- ever) between the formation and expression of an attitude and the opportunity to behave with respect to the attitude object can so easily make for inconsistency between the verbal and the overt behaviours. Research elsewhere in the social sciences shows, moreover, that attitudinal–behavioural consistency is highest when the physical and social situations in which the attitude is verbally expressed are identical to those in which behaviour is subsequently measured.[35] And a strong theme in concomitant consumer research for about a decade has been the direct effect of purchase and consumption situations upon consumer choice behaviour.[36]

It is difficult to avoid the conclusion that situations rather than attitudes are responsible for consumer choice and consumption behaviour. The validity of the idea that persuasive communications cause or modify the formation of attitudes which mediate behaviour, regardless of situation (a concept which is traceable to Allport's pioneering work in social psychology), demands that attitudinal–behavioural consistency be empirically demonstrable under a variety of conditions and circumstances. It is not. Rather the evidence suggests that both attitudinal and behavioural responses vary independently with the situational context in which they are expressed. Here verbal and overt behaviours appear to be controlled by some aspect or other of the situations in which they occur rather than by an underlying psychological variable which, according to the information-processing view, mediates both in a consistent fashion.

Measures of purchase intention based upon verbal responses tend actually to reflect accurately, and consistently (with product classes) patterns of *previous* usage.[37] That these measures of affect or attitude refer to the past rather than the future provides further support for Bem's view that so called attitudinal responses are verbal self-reports of past behaviour in which liking is attributed to (or judged from) observed usage. The evidence presented above favours the 'weak theory of advertising'; it suggests strongly that consumers' experience with the product will reinforce purchase behaviour (positively or negatively) and that repeat buying depends crucially upon the benefits provided by the product in use rather than by 'persuasive' advertising which builds once-and-for-all conviction: as Ehrenberg and Goodhardt[38] sum it up in terms of their ATR model:

'Advertising can first create or strengthen awareness, but often with difficulty. Second, it can help to facilitate a trial purchase, e.g. speed up and ease the launch of a new brand. Third, it can help to reinforce any satisfaction that may occur after use. The advertising does not have to persuade people to buy something that is new to them: it can act as a lubricant, not provide the motive power.'

This reasoning does not, of course, lead to the conclusion that to depict advertising as generally weak is to brand it as invariably ineffectual. At the awareness and reinforcement stages advertising clearly can have unique and far-reaching effects; first, in enabling consumers to discriminate between a new brand and its competitors and secondly, in helping them to recall those benefits in terms which indicate the advertised brand is superior to others. At these times, especially the former, advertising is an indispensable means of communication and attempted influence (albeit at a level of low commitment) and the success of the entire marketing mix depends vitally upon it. But this is far from a vision of advertising as a strongly persuasive force which builds pre-purchase conviction which guarantees brand loyalty. (Indeed, the evidence shows that such loyalty is rarely strong.)[39] Taking the purchase process as a whole, it is product trial and its consequences which emerge as of vital strategic importance to the consumer and the firm: advertising is a means to an end, encouraging the trial of brands and serving to remind the brand's users of its benefits. Advertising attempts to suggest criteria by means of which consumers might choose to discriminate among brands whose differences would otherwise be unapparent to purchasers. The immensity of this task and the failure of so many manufacturers of fast-moving consumer goods to achieve it to their own satisfaction attest to the limited role of advertising and suggest that over the consumers' entire purchase experience with a given brand, advertising performs a relatively minor though essential and indispensable function. This frame of reference leads to the conclusion that if marketing is to succeed, it must do so by the design, creation and distribution of a marketing mix which is comprehensively effective: the most 'persuasive' advertising can bring about at best only one sale per consumer, at least for the most risk-free, relatively inexpensive and probably 'familiar' products. In the absence of the general acceptability of the mix including a product which provides the requisite satis- factions of the criteria the consumer employs to evaluate it, advertising is helpless when it comes to establishing long-term purchasing patterns.

4.5 A behavioural interpretation

The behavioural learning paradigm suggested by the research results reviewed above is not the classical conditioning framework implied in the work of many psychologists, who assumed that the science of human behaviour could be reduced to the study of stimulus-response (S-R) relationships and to processes in which reflexes are conditioned by association. Rather, it is the 'operant' conditioning framework of analysis developed by Skinner and is ultimately founded upon the observation that 'Behaviour is shaped and maintained by its consequences.'[40] A given behaviour (known as an operant because it 'operates upon' the environment) is said to be reinforced by consequences which are such that it is repeated. An important difference between psychologists who belong to this school and those whose framework of conceptualisation and analysis stresses the classical conditioning observed by Pavlov in his canine experiments, is that the former do not generally deny the existence of mental phenomena but question whether such covert events are accessible to scientific analysis. In marketing, it may well be the case that models which present consumer choice processes in terms of hierarchies of psychological effects are relevant to more elaborate cases of consumer decision-making (e.g. with respect to the purchase of a radical and expensive innovation), while the majority of consumer choices, characterised by low-commitment and wide ranges of similar brands are more usefully analysed within a behavioural learning paradigm which focuses on overt, directly observable behaviour (though the division of subject matter on the basis of the applicability of con- ceptualisations and techniques is entirely pragmatic). Thus the selection and use of this or that paradigm is not, in this applied context, a reflection of ultimate beliefs about the nature of human action and its determinants: it is only the selection and use of conceptual frameworks and methods judged appropriate to a task in hand.

The conception employed in the 'strong theory of advertising' and hierarchy of effects models of consumer behaviour is that of an underlying, 'true' attitude which mediates both verbal behaviours made in response to questionnaire 'attitude tests' *and* overt behaviours with respect to the test object, guaranteeing the consistency of the two responses. This underlying attitude is usually conceived as an actual mental event or process though, as has been noted, some psychologists regard it as a hypothetical concept employed to account for the expected attitudinal–behavioural consistency suggested by theories of attitude, which cast it as an inevitable precursor of behaviour regardless of situation. DeFleur and Westie[41] refer to this as the 'latent process conception' of attitude. Its essence is the notion of 'true' attitude which intervenes between some aspect of the environment and the individual's response to it, ensuring the response consistency already noted:

'The attitude is . . . an intervening variable operating between stimulus and response and inferred from the overt behaviour. This inner process is seen as giving both direction and consistency to the person's response.'

As was shown above, the empirical evidence for this proportion is weak in the extreme and suggests therefore that both verbal and overt behaviours are highly situation-specific and that their consistency depends more than anything upon the extent to which the situations in which these responses are given are replicative of each other. Given this evidence, consumer researchers should concentrate upon the investigation of the situational determinants of behaviour:

'A latent something interposed between attitudinal behaviour patterns and the social variables which mediate them is simply unnecessary.'[42]

In view of the failure of the available evidence to sustain the latent process conception of attitude, its alternative, the 'probability conception' of attitude, must surely be adopted. In this, the idea of 'attitudes' denotes the probability that a given behaviour will occur in response to the attitude object in question; observation of previous behaviour in similar contexts provides the material for calculating this relative frequency. 'Attitude' thus reflects the degree of consistency which actually occurs in behavioural responses but the consistency of behaviour is not derived from any process located within the individual's frame of psychological reference and organisation to achieve conformity. Attitude becomes no more than a simple description of behaviour: if consistency is expected or observed, it is because the external, situational contexts over which a series of behaviours is performed correspond, for in such circumstances the contingencies of reinforcement which control behaviour are also constant.

The development of procedures for the analysis of brand purchase sequences is mainly within the spirit of a behaviouristic interpretation. Here the patterns of previous choices, usually unilluminated by the natural detail of marketing activity or indeed the situational context, are the basis for the prediction of subsequent behaviour. In an advertising context such analyses would hope to demonstrate the basis for the regularity of individual and aggregate behaviour, with any departures being traceable to some change in advertising where this can reasonably be presented as the cause of change. Such an approach typically does not overtly depend on *any* psychological mechanism; either some probabilistic interpretation is inferred or the regularity of aggregate behaviour is employed. Some of the stochastic models of brand choice, however, are amenable to a psychological rationale though the questions of inherent, individually-specific mental processes versus the situationally-specific concomitants of choice are thereby introduced. Moreover, the observation of often radically different choice behaviours invites query as to their determinants but evidence of a particular pattern of choice can, nevertheless, support prediction based on this history: such pragmatism may be employed without a full understanding of the reasons for the differences in behaviour. In practice there are formidable technical problems associated with the analysis of brand sequence data and with correlating purchase events with marketing and advertising activity, even disregarding the situation and any underlying psychological processes. The implication of the above discussion is that great and renewed activity to interpret sequence data is necessary and if the explicit detachment from the need to provide a psychological rationale is made, a greater direction to this form of enquiry can be given. The conspicuous need is to achieve a greater relationship between the regularities of such choice behaviour and the contexts in which it occurs.

In the case of low-involvement goods, advertising's weak influence is placed in perspective, but the possibility of other influences has yet to be discussed and the relation of advertising to these assessed. In the remainder of this chapter the role of other inter-personal forms of communication is considered for if these determine behaviour which advertising subsequently reinforces, their nature and the possibility of their control is crucial to advertising success. The question of a change in behaviour arises in a recurrent situation with the introduction of new products; it is especially pertinent, therefore, to consider the role of advertising in these cases.

Buyer-dominated Communication

The fact of inter-personal communication is sufficiently well established in marketing psychology to require little elaboration, but its influence relative to that of marketer-dominated communication is frequently ignored in discussions of the operation and effects of advertising. Lazarsfeld and others[43] drew attention during the 1940s to the tendency of the mass media to communicate information (and thus persuasion) not to the population as a whole so much as to 'opinion leaders' who, in turn, disseminated information and influence by word-of-mouth to the majority of the population. Communication was thus posited to be a two-step process in which most recipients of information effectively ignored the formal mass media and passively received ideas, impressions, data and influence informally from friends, acquaintances and even strangers. Other investigators[44] have advanced the view that consumers tend to be more active than the two-step hypothesis portrays them, assertively seeking information about products, brands and stores from both marketer- and buyer-dominated sources, balancing the costs and benefits of each against those of the other. In any case, empirical studies of consumer influence indicate that the factors and influences which impinge upon buyers are far more complex than either the two-step theory or the atomistic hierarchy of effects models allow. Opinion leaders interact often with each other, for instance, and influence their 'followers' through visual as well as verbal stimuli.[45] Opinion leadership tends to be product-specific and far more pervasive than has hitherto been thought. Rather than search for the characteristics of opinion leaders (e.g. status, interests, communications behaviour) which mark them out as special types of individual, consumer researchers have come to accept that any individual may be a special type of opinion leader given the appropriate circumstances.[46]

Moreover, whether consumers are viewed as essentially active or passive, the examination of advertising and consumer response in terms of observed behaviour rather than assumptions about intra-personal information processing, leads to the conclusion that advertising is a relatively minor source of the pre-purchase information which stimulates trial. Numerous studies indicate the much greater incidence of word-of-mouth rather than formal, mass communication in consumer choice; the extent to which pre-purchase discussion with peers occurs for consumer goods; the positive effects of favourable recommendation of brands and outlets; the tendency of would-be purchasers to consult friends and relatives before choosing (especially) durables; and the circumstances and situations in which opinion leadership operates effectively. The relative effectiveness of marketer-dominated as opposed to buyer-dominated information depends upon a range of situational circumstances which include:

1. The situation in which the innovative purchaser of a radically new consumer product relies exclusively upon marketer-dominated information, simply because the innovative nature of the item precludes its prior use by other customers from whom inter-personal communication might arise: in their time instant coffee, television and home computers have fallen into this category of product.

2. The situation in which the consumer purchases new brands of fast-moving
    goods which involve little if any risk: for instance, razor blades.[47]

While the consumer in the first situation is through lack of substitutes initially
dependent on advertising, the second case permits avoidance of marketer-
dominated communications if these are suspect — though whether his involvement is sufficient to prompt this action and indeed to seek out or absorb inter-
personal communication is another matter. On the other hand, he is likely to
find that interpersonal communication is freely offered in these circumstances
precisely because of the low risk of friendships being harmed if the brand which
is recommended fails to meet the purchaser's expectations, or because the
formulation of advice/information is almost a trivial exercise although one
which is nevertheless of potentially greater value than its 'cost' in a social
context.

The vast majority of purchases of consumer products tend towards the latter
case. From his empirical study of the introduction of stainless steel razor
blades, Sheth[48] has concluded that there is evidence of 'a strong relationship
between awareness from word-of-mouth and influence of word-of-mouth'
which supports his hypothesis that:

'The total market may have a sizeable segment which relies on word-of-mouth
for both information and influence.'

Another finding is that customers whose own trial and adoption behaviours
have been influenced by inter-personal communication are more likely than
other users to stimulate trial on the part of prospective adopters. As the
diffusion process develops and more sceptical consumers are encountered,
buyers require increasing legitimation of the use of the new brand or product in
the form of wide social acceptance rather than advertising claims. Only a
relatively small segment of markets for consumer products are actually
vulnerable to marketer-dominated information and influence: as innovations
are seen by increasing numbers of the population, that influence declines significantly.

Two conclusions may be drawn from this brief summary of the voluminous
research into the sources and effects of information which is dominated by
consumers themselves rather than producers. First, inter-personal communication and influence are ubiquitous facts of consumer life and no account of
consumer behaviour and advertising which ignores them is complete. The
evidence suggests, furthermore, that buyer-dominated communication is
frequently the more persuasive and effective in consumer purchasing.
Secondly, this is entirely consistent with a behaviour-based interpretation of
consumer choice: consumers' reinforcement histories are the logical place to
seek explanations of why they turn repeatedly to given sources of communication or imitate the observed behaviour of given individuals and groups.
Moreover, the frequency of testimonial or celebrity endorsement advertising

copy reflects a recognition of the commercial value of opinion leadership, either through the creation of a social oneness or by emulation and implications of eliteness. Whilst such an approach may on occasions have a relative advantage over other forms of copy, advertising remains a relatively weak source of persuasive consumer communication.

Factors in successful consumer innovation

This conclusion is borne out by consideration of the fates of new consumer products. Authors such as Galbraith, who are preoccupied with the idea that advertising exerts a strong influence on consumers to purchase fashionable brands, overlook the fact that up to 90 per cent of new consumer products fail at the stage of customer acceptance, even with advertising support. Estimates of the rate of new consumer product failure vary according to the objectives of the investigations from which they are derived, their definitions of failure, and the way in which they measure it. But all are consistently high. A British advertising agency which has been involved in a large number of innovative product launches has produced the estimate that only 25 of every 500 new product concepts generated prove worthy of market test, one third of tested brands are launched nationally and, after a decade, one is likely to have remained profitable.[49] Fast-moving consumer innovations have been shown by several British and American investigations to have particularly high failure rates: between 45 and 65 per cent of test-marketed products fail in test and between 10 and 20 per cent of the test survivors are withdrawn subsequent to being made nationally available. Urban and Hauser[50] calculate the probability of successfully marketing a new consumer product at 19 per cent and a director of Unilever has stated that 70 per cent of new food products fail.[51]

Only six or seven major grocery products were annually launched on to the American market with success during the 1960s; the comparable UK figure was two or three. The rate of effective launch declined, moreover, during the 1970s when for the two countries there was a total of four or five successful launches each year.[52] The causes of failure tend to be substantially and increasingly in the product itself and its package rather than in advertising, price or distribution and, while it is notoriously difficult to isolate the effects of a single marketing mix element on sales, it is difficult to avoid the conclusion that most consumer innovations are either judged by buyers to be incapable of delivering the expected benefits or on trial to be disappointing. Successful fast-moving consumer goods, according to a survey by Kraushar[53]:

'tend to be distinctive in some way or other, are in line with general consumer trends, are suitable for the companies making them, and are marketed with a great deal of commitment, singlemindedness and attention to detail.'

Davidson[54] compared fifty successful new grocery brands with fifty which failed and concluded that successful products offered distinct advantages to the consumer in terms of value for money, distinctive benefits and timing. Products which differed little, if at all, from competing brands in terms of value or discernible benefits tended to fail, advertising notwithstanding. Once again it is impossible to avoid the conclusion that, while advertising may play a part in the generation of product trial, adoption depends on the way in which the consequences of product purchase and use reinforce the initial brand choice. And, once again, the tendency is to de-limit sharply our understanding of the nature, scope and effects of advertising. The evidence, whatever it suggests about the need for marketing management to improve its effectiveness, is entirely consistent with the weak theory of advertising and leaves advocates of the strong theory to explain the glaring failure of advertising to create pre-purchase conviction.

4.6 Conclusions

Advertising exerts an effect on consumer behaviour which is generally weak, both absolutely and relative to the remainder of the marketing mix and to that of alternative sources of information and persuasion. The consumer's previous reinforcement pattern, his experience with brands and advertisers, and the situation in which he now purchases constitute the servo-mechanism of influence and it is here that researchers should seek the role of advertising. By and large, advertising does not act forcefully via intra-personal, mental processes to create attitudes which determine behaviour. What emerges inter-estingly from the above account is the tendency of economists, advertisers, marketing managers and the policy makers to cling to the convenient notion that it does. Yet the literature which maintains this simplistic idea, as has been shown, also contains many seeds of doubt which appear to be accumulating to overthrow the information-processing paradigm within marketing thought. Advocates of a behavioural-learning paradigm are being heard more and more. At the very least, theories of how advertising — indeed of how the entire marketing mix — works will have to become far more sophisticated than has hitherto been the case either by embracing the behavioural perspective fully or indicating precisely its sphere of application.

This chapter has made no attempt to philosophise about human nature; nor has it advocated that consumer researchers adopt a behaviouristic framework of conceptualisation and analysis to the exclusion of any other. Rather, it has suggested that, for highly-competitive consumer brands to which consumer commitment is low, the behavioural-learning paradigm provides a more convincing description and explanation of choice and the continuity of consumer behaviour than does the prevailing view based on cognitive learning. The overall conclusion is that, while the aggregate effect of advertising on a materialistic society may be very great, the effectiveness of advertising influence in the case of any particular brand is generally both absolutely and relatively small. This generalisation does not preclude the occasional, specific and limited (often apocryphal) instances where particular conjunctions of advertisements', products' and recipients' inherent characteristics and circumstances permit a greater, if transient, effect. This possibility, whilst not accounting for the maintenance of advertising, does partially explain the often frenetic efforts by advertisers to capture this competitive advantage. A further implication of a behaviouristic interpretation of advertising effects set in a context of non-marketer dominated communication concerns perenially controversial product classes such as alcohol and tobacco. Statistical studies have consistently shown a negligible relationship between advertising and aggregate consumption (competitive advertising is to achieve market share at the expense of rivals), even to the extent that advertising bans have had little effect on consumption. This is not surprising if initial trial of the product and its continuing use is predominantly attributable to social (as opposed to commercial) influence and there is reinforcement in use. If the intention of policy is to curtail consumption then advertising restriction is irrelevant and action to directly reduce consumption or the contexts of its social reinforcement is indicated.

References

1. Colley, R., *Defining Advertising Goals for Measured Advertising Results*, New York: Association of National Advertisers Inc., 1961.
2. *Ibid.*
3. Lavidge, R. J. and Steiner, G. A., 'A Model for Predictive Measurement of Advertising Effectiveness', *Journal of Marketing*, vol. 25, no. 2, 1961, pp.59–62.
4. See, for example, Albion, M. S. and Farris, P. W., *The Advertising Controversy*, Boston, Mass.: Auburn House, 1981, ch. 1.
5. For a basic account, see Atkinson, R. C. and Shiffrin, R. M., 'The Control of Short-Term Memory', *Scientific American*, vol. 225, no. 2, 1971, pp.82–90.
6. Nicosia, F. M., *Consumer Decision Processes*, Englewood Cliffs: Prentice Hall, 1966; Howard, J. A. and Sheth, J. N., *The Theory of Buyer Behaviour*, New York: Wiley, 1969; Engel, J. F., Blackwell, R. D. and Kollat, D. T., *Consumer Behaviour*, Homewood, Illinois: Dryden, 1978; etc.
7. Ehrenberg, A. S. C. and Goodhardt, G. J., 'How Advertising Works', *Essays on Understanding Buyer Behaviour*, New York: J. Walter Thompson Co./Market Research Corporation of America, 1980, pp.2–3.
8. Robertson, T. S., 'A Critical Examination of "Adoption Process" Models of Consumer Behaviour', in Sheth, J. N. (ed.), *Models of Buyer Behaviour*, New York: Harper and Row, 1974, p.282.
9. Howard, J. A., *Consumer Behaviour: Application of Theory*, New York: McGraw-Hill, 1977.

10. Robertson, T. S., 'Low-commitment Consumer Behaviour', *Journal of Advertising Research*, vol. **16**, no. 2, 1976, pp.19–24.
11. *Ibid*.
12. Jacoby, J., Chestnut, R. W. and Silberman, W., 'Brand Choice as a Function of Information Load', *Journal of Consumer Research*, vol **4**, no. 2, 1977, pp.119–28.
13. *Ibid*., p.126, emphasis original.
14. For a more comprehensive discussion, see Foxall, G. R., *Consumer Choice*, London: Macmillan and New York: St. Martins Press, 1983, ch. 4.
15. McConnell, J. D., 'An Experimental Examination of the Price-Quality Relationship', *Journal of Business*, **41**, Oct. 1968, pp.439–44 and Reisz, P. C., 'A Major Price-Perceived Quality Study Re-examined' and 'Comment on "A Major Price Perceived Quality Study Re-examined" ' both in *Journal of Marketing Research*, vol. **17**, May 1980, pp.259–264.
16. Mason, R., 'The Use of Information Sources by Influentials in the Adoption Process', *Public Opinion Quarterly*, vol. **27**, no. 4, 1963, pp.455–466.
17. Ehrenberg, A. S. C., 'Repetitive Advertising and the Consumer', *Journal of Advertising Research*, vol. **14**, no. 2, 1974, pp.25–34.
18. Fishbein, M., 'The Search for Attitudinal-Behavioural Consistency', in Kassarjian, H. H. and Robertson, T. S. (eds.), *Perspective in Consumer Behaviour*, Glenview, Illinois: Scott, Foresman, 1981, p.251.
19. Ray, M. L., 'Marketing Communications and the Hierarchy-of-Effects', in Clarke, P. (ed.), *New Models for Mass Communication Research*, London: Sage, 1973, pp.147–176.
20. *Ibid*., p.151.
21. Festinger, L., *A Theory of Cognitive Dissonance*, Evanston, Illinois: Row, Peterson, 1957.
22. Bem, D., 'Self-perception: An Alternative Interpretation of Cognitive Dissonance Phenomena', *Psychological Review*, vol. **74**, 1967, pp.183–200; and 'Self-perception Theory', in Berkowitz, L. (ed.), *Advances in Experimental Social Psychology*, New York: Academic Press, 1972, pp.1–62.
23. Ray, *op.cit*., p.152, emphasis original.
24. *Ibid*.
25. Krugman, H. E., 'The Impact of Television Advertising: Learning without Involvement', *Public Opinion Quarterly*, vol. **29**, no. 4, 1965, pp.349–356.
26. *Ibid*.
27. Robertson, 'Low-commitment Consumer Behaviour', *op. cit*.
28. Engel, J. F. and Blackwell, R. D., *Consumer Behaviour*, 4th edition, Homewood, Illinois: Dryden, 1982.
29. Olshavsky, R. W. and Granbois, D. H., 'Consumer Decision Making — Fact or Fiction?', *Journal of Consumer Research*, vol. **6**, no. 2, 1979, pp.93–100.
30. Ehrenberg and Goodhardt apparently do not intend that this term be understood in a behaviouristic/operant conditioning sense but it is inter-

esting to note that advertising may well provide this sort of reinforcement.

31. Useful accounts of the science of behaviourism and its philosophy are available in B. F. Skinner's *Beyond Freedom and Dignity*, Harmondsworth: Penguin 1973 and *About Behaviourism*, London: Jonathan Cape, 1974.
32. Wicker, A. W., 'Attitudes vs. Actions: The Relationship of Verbal and Overt Responses to Attitude Objects', *Journal of Social Issues*, vol. **25**, no. 1, 1969, pp.41–78.
33. Fishbein, M., 'Attitude and the Prediction of Behaviour', in Fishbein, M. (ed.), *Readings in Attitude Theory and Measurement*, New York: Wiley, 1967, pp.377–92.
34. Ajzen, I. and Fishbein, M., 'Attitude–Behaviour Relations: A Theoretical Analysis and Review of Empirical Research', *Psychological Bulletin*, vol. **84**, 1977, pp.888–918.
35. See, for example, Norman, R., 'Affective-cognitive Consistency, Attitudes, Conformity and Behaviour', *Journal of Personality and Social Psychology*, vol. **32**, 1975, pp.83–91.
36. See, for example, Belk, W., 'Situational Variables and Consumer Behaviour', *Journal of Consumer Research, vol.* **2**, no. 3, 1975, pp.157–64; Kakkar, P. and Lutz, R. J., 'Situational Influence on Consumer Behaviour: A Review', in Kassarjian and Robertson, pp.204–215; Leigh, J. H. and Martin, C. R., 'A Review of Situational Influence Paradigms and Research', in Enis, B. E. and Roering, K. J. (eds.), *Review of Marketing 1981*, Chicago: A.M.A., 1981, pp.57–74.
37. Ehrenberg, A. S. C. and Goodhardt, G. J., 'Consumer Attitudes', *Essays on Understanding Buyer Behaviour*, New York: J. Walter Thompson Co. and Market Research Corporation of America, 1980.
38. Ehrenberg and Goodhardt, 'How Advertising Works', *op. cit.*, p.5.
39. Ehrenberg, A. S. C., *Repeat Buying*, Amsterdam: North Holland, 1972.
40. Skinner, *Beyond Freedom and Dignity*, p.28.
41. DeFleur, M. L. and Westie, F. R., 'Attitude as a Scientific Concept', *Social Forces*, vol. **42**, no. 1, 1963, pp.17–31.
42. *Ibid.*, p.30.
43. See, for example, Katz, E. and Lazarsfeld, P. F., *Personal Influence*, Glencoe, Illinois: Free Press, 1955.
44. See, for example, Cox, D. F., 'The Audience as Communicators', *Proceedings of the American Marketing Association*, Chicago: A.M.A., 1963.
45. Robertson, T. S., 'Diffusion Theory and the Concept of Personal Influence', in Davis, H. L. and Silk, A. J. (eds.), *Behavioural and Managerial Science in Marketing*, New York: Wiley, 1978, pp.214–36.
46. Foxall, G. R., *Marketing Behaviour*, Aldershot: Gower, 1981, ch. 4.
47. Sheth, J. N., 'Word-of-mouth in Low-Risk Innovations', *Journal of Marketing Research*, vol. **11**, no. 3, 1971, pp.15–18.
48. *Ibid.*, p.16.
49. Davies, B., 'High Risks, Few Winners', *Marketing*, vol. **8**, no. 11, 1982, p.54.

50. Urban, G. L. and Hauser, J. R., *Design and Marketing of New Products*, Englewood Cliffs: Prentice-Hall, 1980, pp.53–5.
51. The *Guardian*, 4 May 1976.
52. Ramsay, W., 'The New Product Dilemma', *Marketing Trends*, no. 1, 1982, pp.4–6; 'New Products in 1981', *Nielsen Researcher*, no. 1, 1982, pp.8–11.
53. Kraushar, P. M., 'Grocers Take Tougher Line', *Marketing*, vol. 8, no. 11, 1982, pp.47–51.
54. Davidson, J. H., 'Why Most New Consumer Brands Fail', *Harvard Business Review*, vol. 54, no. 2, 1976, pp.11–21.

5

Advertising and producer behaviour

5.1 Introduction

In this chapter the process of advertising determination is considered and the nature of and the constraints upon the decisions of advertisers and their advisers are explored. In previous chapters the orientation has been towards the results of advertisers' decisions and the public policy aspects of advertising regulation, both in terms of the maintenance of ethical standards and the curbing of possible abuses of economic power. In part, such issues arise from the actual behaviour of some advertisers, but clearly such policy has also been conceived to prevent abuse and implicitly presumes some standard of acceptable behaviour appropriate to the nature and context of advertising management decisions. Our treatment of policy measures so far has been conducted without elaborating specific features of these decisions, which indeed reflects the manner in which many of the discussions of public policy are conducted. For instance, economic discourse on the subject of advertising regulation is characterised by an abstract and generalised approach to the behaviour of advertisers. It is assumed that they are primarily motivated by the pursuit of optimal profit and that the features of the market structures in which they operate encourage particular forms of behaviour which may lead to undesirable consequences. Advertising in this view is employed to permit the charging of higher prices, and/or to increase the cost of competititon, to deter new entrants or swamp those who cannot afford advertising competition, and/or to supplant rational approaches to product purchase by emotional or insubstantial means either to effect initial sales or to foster loyalty and repeat sales.

The determinism implicit in this view — that advertising *can* and *does* have these effects — is founded neither on empirical evidence nor on appropriate theoretical analysis (see Chapter 2), and it presumes essentially one type of producer behaviour and a compatible single type of consumer response. In Chapter 4 the complexity of consumer response to advertising was demonstrated and this has implications for the producer who must form a view of how recipients respond to advertising amongst other influences in a competitive context. Moreover, as the competitive situation unfolds, with changes in these influences, the producer's view may in turn need modification. A particular form of behaviour based on an unchanging premise cannot be presumed. But, if economics has traditionally focused on the ends of advertisers' behaviour, there are other disciplinary and less specific views which stress the means almost irrespective of the ends; they consider the manifestations of advertising in terms, for instance, of its use of sexual imagery, emotional appeal and possible subliminal influences and the effects it has on the recipients almost in disregard of the particular objectives of advertisers, save that these are commercial ends. Of course, actual producer behaviour cannot divorce the means from the ends and a balanced treatment demands that both aspects are jointly considered.

The advertiser at a particular time attempts to match the characteristics of advertising which are under his control to the requirements of the target audience, in a way appropriate both to this objective and to the competitive and other determinants which define the context in which advertising is selected. To a certain extent this matching process is aided by the accumulation of experience, which supports generalisations of appropriate combinations of product, copy and audience characteristics, and various disciplines contribute concepts and methods to facilitiate the process of simplification and classification. (See Leone and Schultz[1] for a discussion of marketing generalisations.) What is not available, however, is a comprehensive understanding of the means to match advertising to its intended tasks, a lack which renders the advertising decision neither mechanistic nor totally objective. It follows that the form and extent of advertising decisions are heavily influenced by situationally-specific variables. In appreciation of this fact, published works on advertising decision-making adopt either the form of case analysis where the full range of variables and their inter-relationships are explicit, or the principles emerging from case experience or observation form the basis of the generally descriptive, more abstract approach which encourages a uni-disciplinary approach with the orientation and specialisation which this inevitably entails. Possibly the most eclectic treatment of the advertising decision is to be found in the marketing literature and this influence is prominent in this chapter, which considers the setting of advertising objectives, budgeting, optimal advertising, pragmatic and competitive behaviour, and advertiser relationships to the media.

5.2 Objectives and implementation

Whatever may be the ultimate objective of advertising and its contribution to the firm's purposes, there is necessarily a variety of instrumental objectives which must first be achieved. Indeed, it is primarily these instrumental objectives which determine the characteristics of advertising and account for the ways in which the advertising budget is conceived and spent. The importance of instrumental objectives is apparent from the fact that only in comparatively rare instances is advertising an *end* in itself; certainly there are occasions when the desire just to be an advertiser is paramount — for example, where the form of advertisement serves the fancy of a company chairman, or where just to employ a particular medium has a certain cachet — but in the vast majority of cases advertising is conducted not as an end in itself but as a means to some end or ends, and before any final objective can be attained there may be several intermediate objectives to be secured. Frequently, ultimate objectives are not — indeed cannot — be defined in more than the vaguest terms and in this event instrumental objectives come to be treated as ultimate ends. This arises for several reasons:

1. Departmental interpretation of higher management's outline proposals either in terms of the communication brief or budget involves a process with its own momentum and criteria from which refined objectives are eventually discerned.
2. The essentially creative nature of advertising precludes the articulation of precise objectives prior to work on the advertisements themselves; in effect it is from particular advertisements that objectives arise.
3. Comparatively little is known about the mechanisms which translate advertisements into behavioural responses.
4. Advertising objectives are contingent on other aspects of the firm's activity and on decisions which may yet be pending or awaiting fulfilment.
5. The purpose of setting objectives may be primarily to effect control and this requirement leads to the framing of objectives in more specific terms.

Some indication of the scope available for the conception of intermediate objectives is given by Colley's[2] list of more than 50 such objectives, but there is no reason to think that this is exhaustive and multiple objectives formed by combinations may also be entertained. (See also Corkindale and Kennedy.[3]) Such objectives may be expressed in terms of communication criteria in either qualitative or quantitative terms, for instance, achieving a particular number of aided/unaided recalls or giving some particular proportion of a potential audience a specified number of opportunities to see advertisements. Altern- atively, the objective may be couched in terms of some behavioural response — return of coupons, enquiries, orders placed or stockists gained, for instance. In some cases the achievement of such instrumental objectives — chosen for their tractability — may bear a clear relationship to the ultimate company objec- tives, expressed in terms of profitability, stability, growth, survival etc., *if* these are sufficiently explicit. In general though, the contribution of advertising alone will be obscured by a host of intervening variables or be diffused over time or products in ways that are imperfectly understood and, accordingly, unquantifiable.

Where advertising is not employed as a communications end in itself, its effects are necessarily achieved in combination with other aspects of the product — its price, distribution or context and the other forms of communication impinging on customers, whether these are controlled by the firm or not. The setting of advertising in a marketing context, where these other elements of the marketing mix besides advertising combine into an integrated whole, makes the isolation of purely advertising objectives problematical. Advertising is employed to complement other aspects of the mix. Its contribution to the promotion of a new product is a conspicuous example but the notification of distributive availability, price or special features or services frequently occurs. The instrumental communication objectives may be routinely set and monitored, but the contribution of advertising to, for example, sales or profit — which may be its ultimate purpose — cannot generally be distinguished from the contribution to this outcome from product features, attractive price, or whatever. There are, however, occasions when advertising is the only variable to be changed and if this is specific to one product and defined objective then its contribution may be isolated. For example, in comparative test marketing situations where other factors are standardised or even controlled and multivariate statistical analysis might also be employed, to which the discussion will return.

The firm's strategic purposes may be satisfied if advertising is employed to meet, or be compatible with, several instrumental objectives. Thus a contribution from advertising to profit, sales targets or whatever can be made in a host of different fashions, for instance through the mechanisms of attitude change, information provision or image creation. But, whilst an advertisement or campaign may be conceived with a particular mechanism in mind, beneficial or adverse effects can arise from other mechanisms. It is certainly unrealistic to assume that only one effect, let alone the intended one, is likely to be the sole mechanism operative between the advertiser and a large and diffuse audience whose members all have different circumstances and perceptions.

This point may be illustrated with one of the models of the advertising process discussed in Chapter 4: the Lavidge and Steiner[4] model portrays advertisements achieving a hierarchy of effects from awareness → knowledge → liking → preference → conviction prior to purchase. Advertisements would in general inevitably have some effect on creating awareness (though there is the possibility that the advertisement could become so familiar that it could fail to secure the minimal objective), but a more informative advertisement aimed at establishing knowledge, following those designed primarily to achieve recognition or awareness, still retains the capacity to create awareness or indeed to facilitate any of the other stages in the process. Moreover, even if the model is assumed to be generally valid, some advertising recipients undoubtedly purchase within, rather than at the end of a sequence, or indeed purchase can occur for entirely unrelated reasons. It is the case that there is neither comprehensive knowledge of the possible mechanisms which mediate advertisements and response thereto nor the capability to match advertisements unambiguously to those mechanisms that have been mooted, and in this situation the advertiser is in part dependent on serendipity. In the absence of a single definitive mechanism which the advertiser can presume, advertisements are designed to operate on a variety of levels whose common feature is the avoidance of negative effects. Because the advertiser is necessarily parading his own interest, even if this is also to the consumer's benefit — and advertisements to some extent require an expenditure of time and effort on the part of the recipient — the avoidance of net negative effects is attempted in a variety of ways. This includes the obvious professionalism and attention to detail but also the alignment of the ingredients of the advertisement to the intended audience. Thus humour, association, celebrity presence, or whatever feature in the advertisement fulfils the intended minimal function of providing something positive for the recipient in compensation for his time and effort. Of course these features are intended to complement the overall message/product to give greater positive benefit as a first step towards eliciting a favourable response in return.

Arising from the uncertainties associated with advertising, advertisers have frequently been loath to specify both ultimate and instrumental objectives because their role as meaningful targets cannot be fulfilled. Undoubtedly, as many have noted (e.g. Majaro[5] and Colley[6]), it would be advantageous to specify objectives so that advertising effectiveness may be assessed and advertising thereby improved, but this is to mistake the essential difficulty of applying this management nostrum to the peculiarities of advertising, at least within current levels of knowledge. The objectives defined and worked to are rather to be seen as control and communication devices to co-ordinate and monitor performance of the advertising function in isolation. The recognition of the need to utilise advertising at all, to employ advertising strategically, gives rise to a set of other requirements entailing the management of advertising within its pre-specified or jointly determined parameters and thus to its co-ordination with other aspects of the firm's marketing activities.

5.3 Budgeting for advertising

The uncertainty and lack of specificity in the determination of advertising objectives is reflected in the ways firms make their advertising appropriations. As revealed by many surveys (e.g. Taplin,[7] Rees,[8] Augustine and Foley[9]), and enshrined in textbooks, a series of methods or rationales are widely in use but at the same time there is a recurrent lament about the lack of 'sophistication' in the methods used which can be initially listed as follows:

1. Competitive parity: matching competitor's expenditures level.
2. What can be afforded or intuitively justified.

3.   Percentage of sales.
4.   Objective and task.

In due course aspects of these methods are discussed, but a prior requirement is to consider what is (or should be) included in the advertising budget. Some insight into why this should be necessary follows from the attempt by *Printers' Ink*[10] in 1960 to obtain agreement among survey respondents on which 81 classes of expense (each of which includes a wide range of items) could reasonably be classified as advertising expenditure. Different support was found amongst firms for particular items and accordingly types of expenditure were classified as 'white', 'grey' and 'black' charges depending respectively on whether more than two-thirds, between one-third and two-thirds, or less than one-third respondents agreed that items were appropriately designated. Updating this study in 1981 Patti and Blasko[11] found significant change in the composition of agreement, thus the *Printers' Ink* list of fifteen white charges was reduced by one half. This indicates a growing specialisation in the definition of advertising and perhaps a refinement of the job responsibilities of particular respondents. In practice, working definitions of classes of advertising expenditure and ultimately of the domain of advertising decision-making in general are attuned to particular purposes or to the requirements of a particular viewpoint — accountancy conventions and advertising definitions for disciplinary purposes are cases in point. Nevertheless, classificatory problems abound. For instance, many economists employ the term 'advertising' as indicative of non-production expenses; they generalise advertising to include sales promotions, publicity, and other categories of communications expenses which marketers and advertisers would sharply distinguish. But even with a distinction drawn between say advertising as 'paid-for time' and publicity as 'not directly paid-for time', inevitably publicity is 'managed' and incurs expenses which blur its distinctive characteristics for budgetary purposes.

Individual firms must each necessarily decide their own treatment of various categories of expenditure and determine the period to which the spending plans refer. Difficulties arise here from the composition of the firm's product portfolio, its organisational structure and the nature of its advertisements which can be briefly illustrated. For instance, some advertising employed by a company may refer to all or several of its products whilst other messages are product specific; likewise, the time frame to which advertisements are designed may be different for various purposes — clearly the 'image' type of advertising has a longer relevance than an announcement for imminent effect. The practice in some cases is to determine an overall advertising budget for later disaggregation and allocation to products, area, media, etc. Whilst in others the organisation cumulates product and other advertising requirements to arrive at an overall figure. Rees,[12] for instance, found that 90 per cent of his sample firms did the latter.

The attribution of advertising expenditure to product and time is accordingly rarely a straightforward matter and inevitably arbitrary or conventional allocations occur. Against this background the 'unscientific' allocation of advertising monies is not surprising and, of course, the evolution of budgetary procedures is in response to the realities of experience which, whilst not infallible or necessarily satisfatory, cannot be lightly dismissed. Moreover, the conventional methods as listed above are but a short description of an orientation to budgetary practice which differs widely in implementation and in the requirements of particular products, contexts and time. These methods are not necessarily employed from complacency about the pursuit of efficiency in advertising but from a realisation that significantly greater precision is unachievable. This is consistent in turn with advertisers' experience and beliefs that marginal changes in advertising expenditure levels or tactics are likely to have undetectable effects and that, although large changes would be more likely to have an effect, the risk is not to be undertaken lightly. Also, because advertising complements other aspects of the firm's marketing mix, there are limits to the practicality of altering advertising on an *ad hoc* basis by significant amounts. Rather, such changes must arise from the reappraisal of marketing strategy as a whole.

There is an additional reason which imposes limits upon the flexibility of advertising and which is especially pertinent to large advertisers. The budget amount must, of course, be spent but there are rigidities in the organisation of the production and transmission of advertising. Magazine space and prime television time in particular must be booked several months in advance and whilst some advertising media can be deployed at short notice, this capability is of only marginal significance to large advertisers. The conventional annual budgeting cycle may lack a purely logical basis and on occasions impede the flexible use of advertising, but such fears have probably been exaggerated and the annual or some periodic cycle is necessary to facilitate the organisation of advertising, both for advertising management and in the firm at large. Likewise, the comparative stability of advertising budgets that arises from the utilisation of the affordable, or percentage of sales methods in the relatively static markets for mature products also reflects a concern with the requirements for orderly planning, ordering and control, rather than with the effects or effectiveness of advertising which follows at a later time. Despite these considerations, there is consensus that the most logical method of determining the advertising appropriation is by the 'objective and task' method. This envisages that the unique qualities of advertising are selected for specific purposes and accordingly there are interrelated decisions about the timing, copy, media allocation, frequency, reach, and a matching of the advertising plans to the competitive context and to what can be afforded. In short, the comprehensive implementation of the objective and task method replaces its alternatives. The impediments to its use are limitations on the knowledge of how particular advertising works and the attendant difficulties of defining objectives: it is of practical significance only in specific circumstances and not necessarily appropriate for recurrent or frequent cases confined to instrumental objectives.

Whether advertising budgeting, within the time and institutional constraints in which it operates, can be significantly improved in a cost-effective manner depends on the theoretical perspective of how this might be achieved and also crucially on the availability and analysis of requisite data. These matters lead to the consideration of *optimal* advertising which is a topic which many economists, advertising researchers and marketers (who are not usually intellectual allies) have made common cause.

5.4 Optimal advertising

Interest in the optimality of advertising arises in several contexts often closely related to disciplinary concerns, but the aspect of advertising which is either to be optimised or whose optimality is to be assessed, must be carefully distinguished. The most frequent usages refer to the optimality of the advertising budget, the optimal allocation of the given budget, the optimal allocation of a media budget over different vehicles and the question of the optimality of advertising in the economy. In each case, the logic of optimality is more easily conceived than implemented, though inevitably the interest and ability to conceive of optima is related to the availability of mathematical/statistical technique. The treatment here is primarily of the optimal budget though some of this analysis is tangentially applicable to the question of the optimality of advertising in the economy.

Both theoreticians and practitioners have devoted considerable effort to the analysis of advertising expenditure with the objective of optimising profit. Thus optimal advertising is (usually) conceived in terms of the sales revenue inducing effect on the one hand and its cost on the other. Maximum profit is achieved when the marginal revenue stemming from advertising is just equal to the marginal cost incurred in advertising; at lower levels of advertising some revenue-inducing potential has been forgone whilst, if the marginal cost of advertising exceeds the revenue accruing from it, that advertising expenditure would be 'wasted' and better allocated elsewhere. This marginalist logic has been the underlying principle in the development of a number of theoretical models specifying the rules for optimal advertising expenditure. These rules are derived from the analysis of carefully specified situations of increasing complexity following the initial work by Rasmussen[13] and Dorfman and Steiner.[14]

Dorfman and Steiner considered the profit-maximising advertising expenditure for a monopolist under static conditions of known demand. Specifying the demand function (Q) in terms of price (P) and advertising (A):

$Q=Q(P,A)$, the rules for the optimal advertising expenditure may be expressed in either of two ways:

1   Advertising should be increased to the point where its marginal sales effectiveness equals the price elasticity of demand (e)

$$P\frac{\partial Q}{\partial A}=e$$

2   The advertising sales ratio should equal the ratio of advertising elasticity of demand (a) to the price elasticity of demand (e)

$$\frac{A}{PQ}=\frac{a}{e}$$

where $a=\dfrac{\partial Q}{\partial A}\cdot\dfrac{A}{Q}$ and $e=-\dfrac{\partial Q}{\partial P}\cdot\dfrac{P}{Q}$

More elaborate models allowing variously and in combination for the effects of advertising and price over time and the responses of competititors have been constructed by Nerlove and Arrow,[15] Schmalensee,[16] and by Cowling *et al.*[17] From these models, the profit maximising rules show remarkable similarity to rule (2) above if advertising and price elasticities are appropriately defined. Thus, what might be called the *generic* Dorfman-Steiner rules state that optimum advertising requires that the advertising sales ratio should equal the ratio of (adjusted) advertising and price elasticities of demand. Indeed this basic form is appropriate for the maximisation of managerial utility (Peel[18]) and market share (Lambin[19]). The comparative simplicity of these theoretical rules and their superficial conformity with the widely-practised rule of thumb methods of setting advertising appropriations as a percentage of sales has led to many attempts to 'apply' the above theories to empirical situations. Indeed, the formulation of some of the theoretical specifications leading to the generic Dorfman-Steiner rules were guided by the desire to achieve greater realism in the way advertising affects sales and in modelling the competitive context in which advertising decisions occur.

An early cautionary note was, however, forwarded by Dorfman and Steiner:[20]

'There are good grounds for doubting the economic significance of the whole business of writing down profit functions (or drawing curves) and finding points of zero partial derivatives (or graphical points of tangency). Such devices are merely aids to thinking about practical problems and it may be an uneconomical expenditure of effort to devote too much ingenuity to developing them. Yet such devices are aids to clear thought and, if sufficiently simple and flexible, they help us find implications, interrelationships, and sometimes contradictions which might escape notice without them.'

In investigating the significance of the generic Dorfman-Steiner rules beyond the confines of a purely theoretical perspective, it is necessary to consider the nature of the tests of the theory and its subsequent performance. This involves matters of some complexity, especially where different criteria support differing conclusions and where the trade-offs between such criteria involve fine judgement. Nevertheless, because the generic Dorfman-Steiner rules and their associated empirical procedures have been advocated firstly for the determination of optimal advertising expenditures (by advertising researchers, agencies, managerial economists and marketers, e.g. Dhalla[21] and Broadbent[22]), for primarily commercial purposes and secondly for use in the assessment of advertising expenditures for economic purposes to support particular positions in the debate about the need for quantitative regulation of advertising expenditures, it is appropriate to consider the issues in some detail, under a number of headings.

Assumptions

The objective of profit maximisation is explicit assumption of the models but in the various specifications the nature of the included and omitted variables, the treatment of time and the conception of consumers' behaviour, the competitive and organisational context, all involve additional assumptions many of which are implicit. Obviously, the various models that comprise the generic category exhibit different attributes but some general features may nevertheless be discerned. To include advertising in expenditure form is to treat it homogeneously and this is no less the case with treatments which distinguish *messages* from *expenditures* and therefore allow for the *price* but not the *content* of advertisements – see Schmalensee[23] — but to disregard the nature of advertising copy is critical. The models also typically assume that there is a (costless) optimisation of advertising expenditures over media and time.

A certain determinism in the way advertising leads to sales revenues is implied — it is as if the mere act of buying advertising buys customers, rather than the advertising messages in their qualitative aspects contributing to purchase behaviour in a variety of ways through different and vicarious mechanisms. Formulations in aggregate objective terms are unable to capture the essential subjectivity of advertising reception, thus the use of an objective quantity concept denies the conjunction of that reception with the physical product itself into a composite which is the actual entity purchased when advertising has had an effect.

The formulations showing advertising in monetary terms with an objective product definition are better suited to the analysis of advertising purely as information and thus separate from the product purchase decision in both time and cost dimensions (see Chapter 3), but they are in keeping with their genesis to the extent that econometrics is based on economic theory. On the other hand, the lack of specificity in the way advertising expenditure leads to sales permits the possibility of *any* acceptable composite arising from the conjunction of advertising and the physical product but this, of course, begs the question of the formulation of the appropriate copy and the management of advertising to achieve such effects in the first instance.

In a further respect, the representation of advertising in expenditure terms alone may be appropriate. Thus where a manufacturer gives advertising support to a product to establish its 'credibility' in the eyes of the consuming public and more especially in relation to the purchasing decisions of distributors, the amount of expenditure rather than the way in which (within broad limits) that expenditure is allocated is the significant point of advertising. Most applications of the generic Dorfman-Steiner models, however, omit consideration of the behaviour of distributors and are conceived in terms of final demand only. Distributive characteristics, somewhat belatedly, are gaining recognition in economics literature, at least in distinguishing broad categories of copy, thus retailers' advertising is seen as broadly informative with manufacturers' being persuasive, e.g. Boyer,[24] and indirectly the different advertising sales ratios associated with different products are recognised as indicative of alternative marketing characteristics (including channels of distribution) rather than purely the outcome of market power, e.g. Porter.[25]

Time Considerations

The models which incorporate some adjustment process of demand to advertising over time recognise a variety of features of both advertising and consumers' behavioural patterns. For instance:

1. Advertising must cumulate over time to reach thresholds of effectiveness.
2. Current advertising recipients are not necessarily current consumers, the advertising influence will occur later.
3. Advertising inculcates habits which further advertising maintains.
4. Advertising is subject to obsolescence and wear-out and needs renewal.

Despite this variety, the methods used to incorporate time effects do not distinguish between these various features although in principle they could do. Rather, the recognition of time effects is used to support the proposition that advertising expenditures should be regarded in terms of investment principles and expressed in dynamic formulations. An influential approach by Nerlove and Arrow[26] conceives that current advertising contributes to a stock of advertising influence — goodwill — which is a determinant of sales. Current advertising can increase the stock of goodwill or maintain its level given that it depreciates at a constant rate. To maximise profits the appropriate levels and paths of both price and advertising must be determined, which depends on the certain response of consumers and a constancy of the interest rate on advertising funds. It may be shown that the optimal advertising to sales ratio is a function of appropriately adjusted elasticities of advertising and price and the instantaneously optimal policy is the dynamic counterpart of the Dorfman-Steiner theorem, a result which depends on the assumption that the stock of goodwill can be maintained at constant cost. Nerlove and Arrow[27] themselves consider this 'is actually very unrealistic' since at high levels of advertising expenditure there must be resort to inferior media etc. which must raise the cost of maintaining goodwill. The Nerlove and Arrow conception of a depreciating stock of goodwill dependent on the current and past levels of advertising outlays, adjusted in conformity with current sales, is equivalent to a Koyck type of distributive lag model where current advertising depends on current sales and the advertising in the preceding period alone — see Koutsoyiannis.[28]

The properties of the Koyck system, to enable the truncation of a possibly long prior sequence of influences on current events, have been especially prized by empirical researchers. In the case of advertising, if the effects of previous advertising on current sales could be assumed to be declining geometrically, then the current and past effects of advertising on sales could be distinguished and (subject to further considerations) empirically determined. Indeed, the utilisation of such a distributive lag system in conjunction with the Dorfman-Steiner theorem in a pioneering study by Palda[29] set a basic methodology for the establishment of optimal advertising policy which, because of its importance, is considered in more detail below.

Where time is recognised as an important component in models of optimal advertising determination and especially in empirical work, it is appropriate that separate functions should describe how advertisers respond to unfolding events and how advertising influences consumer demand. If advertising influences sales which in turn contribute to the advertising decision then a simultaneous equation system is indicated. Certainly, where there is an underlying simultaneous system, attempts to estimate the parameters of a single equation model by ordinary least squares are likely to yield biased and inconsistent estimates of the coefficients. This has prompted some attempts to employ simultaneous equation estimation techniques in the acquisition of price and advertising elasticities, but a conspicuous overall superiority of such models has not been demonstrated and despite its theoretical limitations the single equation mode continues to predominate. This in part accounts for the tendency of most studies to be concerned with the effects of advertising on demand and to take the level of advertising as given, a posture which ignores producer decision-making. Interest then centres on whether the level is appropriate for optimal profit. This indeed was the approach adopted by Palda, whose data on the Lydia Pinkham Company has, incidentally, been extensively re-analysed in the quest for a more refined estimation procedure.

Assessing Optimal Advertising Expenditures

A simplified specification of the relationships from which the parameter estimates that are necessary to make the general Dorfman-Steiner rules operational is given below. This provides a basis for a subsequent discussion on the efficacy of this approach to optimal budgeting, though our simplification omits econometric simplification. Palda employed the Koyck distributive lag system whereby the effect of previous advertising on current sales geometrically declines by a factor $\lambda(0<\lambda<1)$, the further in the past that advertising expenditure occurred. Thus

$$S_t = a_o + a_1 A_t + a_1 \lambda A_{t-1} + a_1 \lambda^2 A_{t-2} + a_1 \lambda^3 A_{t-3} + \ldots$$

and lagging by one period and multiplying by λ

$$\lambda S_{t-1} = a_o \lambda + a_1 \lambda A_{t-1} + a_1 \lambda^2 A_{t-2} \ldots$$

Finding $S_t - \lambda S_{t-1}$ and re-arranging

$$S_t = a_o(1-\lambda) + a_1 A_t + \lambda S_{t-1} \tag{1}$$

In effect the entire set of previous advertising influences is summarised in the λS_{t-1} term — the lagged dependent variable — in (1).

From (1) the short run and long run marginal sales effectiveness of advertising may be obtained.

$$\text{SRMSE} = \frac{dS_t}{dA_t} = a_1$$

$$\text{LRMSE} = \sum_{t=0}^{\infty} a_1 \lambda^t = \frac{a_1}{1-\lambda}$$

As stated above, the Dorfman-Steiner result gives as the condition for optimal advertising that the marginal sales effectiveness of advertising should equal the price elasticity of demand, that is, $\text{MSE} = e$.

Palda did not have direct estimates of (e) for Pinkham's but employing the theoretical proposition that it is irrational for a profit-maximising monopolist to produce where $e < 1$ ($\text{MR} < 0$) it could therefore be deduced that only LRMSE was compatible with profit maximisation since $\text{SRMSE} < 1$ and $\text{LRMSE} > 1$. Some corroboration of this interpretation is obtained from application of the proposition that an optimal pricing policy has the mark-up equal to the reciprocal of (e) and in Pinkham's case this approximately equated with LRMSE. Thus assuming that optimal pricing was employed, optimal advertising was also achieved. The consistency of these deductions enabled some confidence to be placed in the parameter estimates (in addition to econometric justification) — especially in the estimates of MSE and λ. Indeed, by knowledge of these estimates and the mark-up (c) the marginal rate of return on advertising investment (r) may be calculated.

$$r = \frac{ca_1 + \lambda - 1}{1 - ca_1}$$

and by considering a proportion ($x\%$) of the total sales-generating capacity of advertising the $x\%$ life of advertising may be deduced. That is, the time (t) for advertising to exhaust $x\%$ of its effect is

$$\frac{S(t)}{S(\infty)} = x$$

where $S(t)$ is the sum of the geometric progression of MSE terms for (t) periods and $S(\infty)$ is its sum to infinity. (In Pinkham's case the 95 per cent life of advertising was approximately 7 years — from $.05 = 1 - \lambda^t$.)

In this study, Palda essentially accepted the validity of the Dorfman-Steiner theory which he then applied and this confirmed his acceptance, because a coherent set of economically acceptable estimates were obtained which found some further theoretical corroboration. On this basis the theory was not subjected to definitive test and although dozens of studies employed Palda's basic methodology (with varying success), there are a number of qualifications which do limit its application to the determination of the optimal budget.

Specification problems

Earlier mention has been made of the theoretical requirement for the function which shows the relationship of sales to advertising expenditure to be compatible with the way in which advertising is determined. Advertising is not exogeneously determined but reflects the decisions of management. Where there is a simultaneous relationship between sales and advertising then the advertising function must be specified as well. In the case of the Pinkham's data, Schmalensee[30] investigated the variability of the rate of return implied by the parameter estimates in Palda's equation and concluded from their erratic pattern that:

'Clearly, either Pinkham's management did not view the firm's demand function as Palda described it, or they behaved in a consistent yet irrational manner for over half a century.'

Thus the original Palda equation judged on the basis of certain econometric tests and its compatibility with the Dorfman-Steiner theory is found wanting against a different test of its efficacy. Moreover, subsequently other criticisms and inconsistencies have become apparent.

Some insight into the issues involved may be seen if we consider the following illustrative specification.

$$S_t = k + bA_t + \varrho S_{t-1} + cA_{t-1} \tag{2}$$

Depending on the values of the parameters this specification can represent quite different versions of the advertising sales relationship. For instance

1. If $c = 0$ the specification is equivalent to (1) and may depict the Koyck-type distributed lag advertising pattern.
2. If $b = c = 0$ current and immediately prior advertising have no discernible effect on sales. If $b > 0$ and $c = 0$ only current advertising affects sales and $MSE = b$. In either case the ϱS_{t-1} term may be interpreted as an adjustment of previous sales without any advertising implication.
3. If $c = -\varrho b$ it is implied that advertising has *only* current effects. This may be seen by presuming $S_t = k + bA_t$ and by lagging and multiplying by ϱ, $\varrho S_{t-1} = k\varrho + b\varrho A_{t-1}$ which on substitution in (2) leaves sales equal to a constant plus the current effects of advertising.

In fact several more versions can be obtained from (2) and these and a discussion of econometric considerations are to be found in Clarke[31] and Weiss and Windal.[32] It was Clarke who raised questions on whether the cumulative effects methodology employed initially by Palda but adopted subsequently by others was in fact giving spurious results. Clarke noticed that the estimates of the coefficient of the lagged sales variable, for data intervals of different durations, gave inconsistent results for the life of advertising. Thus in the Pinkham's case and in others the implied life of advertising was greater when annual data rather than monthly or quarterly data was employed although, of course, as a matter of arithmetic the estimates should tally. From a review of dozens of studies he concluded that the 'duration intervals derived from annual models are too long'; indeed, he found that:

'the average implied duration interval derived from annual data is more than 17 times as long as the implied duration interval derived from monthly data'.[33]

For frequently-bought consumer goods the 90 per cent life of advertising was estimated to be between three and nine months. This in turn suggests that at least in terms of annual data a current effects model is appropriate and indeed Clarke found some evidence supporting the interpretation in 3 above. Whilst the question of data interval bias must be recognised some of the conclusions reached by Clarke — especially in the case of the Pinkham's data — have been challenged by Weiss and Windal,[34] who find counter evidence on the basis of revised estimation techniques for the retention of *some* cumulative effects of advertising.

The question of whether a current effects or a cumulative effects model is adopted is, however, *crucial* to a test of the optimality of advertising employing the Dorfman-Steiner results. As shown above, the estimates of SRMSE and LRMSE differ only by a factor of $\frac{1}{1-\lambda}$ but if λ does *not* refer to a distribution of lagged advertising effects, the utilisation of λ for such a purpose is improper and the calculations of rate of return, advertising durability etc. are *invalid*. Moreover, the Dorfman-Steiner result, when appropriate, indicates for MSE > e that *both* price and advertising should be increased and for MSE < e that *both* variables should be decreased for greater profit. Clearly if the estimates employed are deficient, prescriptions counter productive to the profit objective would be indicated. Whilst this can occur because of the interpretation of advertising-related parameters, a similar problem can arise from imprecision of estimates of the price elasticity of demand. Palda's study of the Pinkham's data was by no means exceptional in *deducing* the value of e on the assumption that optimal pricing was conducted. (Why *optimal* pricing should be presumed as a basis for the assessment of advertising policy rather than *vice versa* is a moot point). Ideally, estimates of (e) that are compatible with advertising estimates and refer to particular time periods on a commensurate basis in terms of lag structures are required. Typically, however, difficulties do arise due to specification problems, data availability or limitations of estimation technique. The net result according to Scheidell[35] is that:

'Very few empirical studies of advertising are designed to estimate demand as a function of price and advertising and none is in a form that specifies the relation between advertising and short and long run elasticities.'

Scheidell[36] contributes a further point of reservation concerning the indication of a price or advertising change based on the Dorfman-Steiner condition, when he argues that application of the static prescription can lead to a result opposite from the one intended if there are lags in consumers' response to a change in price. Thus where a reduced price is indicated to increase profits, although this result will eventually ensue, in the shorter term there can be losses as the expected increase in sales has yet to materialise whilst existing sales are less profitable than hitherto. Such consideration should bias the firm towards the smaller price reduction.

'Also, if the demand is sufficiently large, it should bias the firm towards price increases, when static analysis would otherwise suggest the price decrease.'

Conclusions on optimal advertising

The theoretical analysis of optimal budgeting yields a number of results expressing the optimal advertising expenditure as a proportion of sales in terms of appropriately defined advertising and price elasticities of demand — this theory is specified for a range of competitive conditions and time periods. The theory has possible applications in two principal directions. Firstly, it may be employed by the advertiser to check the optimality of previous advertising as a guide to improved decisions in the future. Secondly, such an analysis of private profitability, where perhaps 'excessive' advertising is demonstrated, can prove of interest to economic regulators concerned on the public's behalf with the allocation of resources. Furthermore, to the extent that a generalised experience of brand and product elasticities is acquired by replication of the technique for a variety of different advertising themes, then the inherent inability of the models to portray qualitative effects is mitigated to some degree (although the incorporation of dummy variables to capture the effects of advertising copy or media changes has occurred in some cases). Of course, even the perfect under-standing of the past is of uncertain efficacy as a guide to future behaviour and for a large number of reasons the methodology described above falls short of such a standard.

Crucially, the isolation of advertising's effect from other influences on sales must be established. In the absence of experimental control the task is to untangle, by multi-variate statistical methods, the various contributions of those variables thought to be operative. The Pinkham's case was a particularly simple one in this respect because advertising was predominantly used but nevertheless specification problems concerning the contribution of variables still arose. In general, because of the complexity of short term influences, longer period analyses are favoured to reduce the 'noise' of miscellaneous influences, so that salient features may be seen in greater focus. This is admirable where the phenomena to be analysed can naturally be partitioned in such a fashion, but in the case of advertising this is often not the case as shown by Clarke. Qualitative changes in copy, media allocations and audience characteristics are frequent, with intervals to be measured in weeks rather than years, and what the analyst may wish to classify as 'noise' may be the essential phenomena integral to the analysis. In effect, there is a distinct possibility that the analyses are conducted at too general a level, disproportionate to the complexity of the phenomena to which they refer, e.g. the characteristics of advertising are subsumed in advertising expenditure, the period of influence is arbitrarily imposed, competitive advertising is merely expenditure, etc. The application of such methods to shorter periods is in turn impeded by the acquisition of appropriate data involving the structure and co-operation of distribution channels, where the sheer scale of operations is relevant to this. Yet the choice of period for the analysis data is *fundamental* to the application of the relevant theory, and the evolving experience from the intensive analysis of particular sets of data (Pinkham's, for instance) shows that the application of the methodology to any new set is inherently problematic. Certainly, the apparent simplicity and plausibility of the theory is compro-mised by the considerable difficulty and complexity of implementing it and interpreting the results. Moreover, it is *still* debated whether the Pinkham's data are consistent with the pursuit or the achievement of optimal advertising at least 20 years from the initial investigation. The essential technical characteristics of this debate must be set against the purposes which initially inspired it: the quest for optimal advertising budgets. The apparent theoretical endorsement of the advertising sales ratio has been cited as a justification for the rules of thumb method widely employed — Schmalensee[37] and Broadbent.[38] This is merely incidental when so much imprecision attends the conceptualisation and determination of the relevant price and advertising elasticities, and where these are unlikely to be constant in the face of evolving market competitive conditions. Inevitably, advertising expenditure can be expressed as a proportion of sales but whether that ratio is optimal is dependent on a wider knowledge than the above methodology encompasses and, in general, the fundamental impediment to the determination of optimal advertising remains the familiar one of the lack of an adequate conceptualisation of how advertising works.

5.5 Pragmatism in advertising

Where commercial advertising research must be cost-effective, it is not surprising that research inputs have been concentrated on the more tangible aspects of the production and transmission of advertising, with the specifics of media allocation, positioning, duration, frequency, size of advertisements, type of copy, etc., and addressed to such features on a single rather than a holistic basis. Moreover, the research is necessarily small-scale and predominantly concerned with the choice between formulated alternatives prior to transmission rather than the creation of alternatives or the examination of post-display effects. The research is primarily to avoid the potential negative effects that inappropriate advertising might elicit rather than the creation of positive attributes, and the monitoring of advertising effects through consumer research has a similar broad intention. This emphasis arises from the boundless creative possibilities that are inherent in advertising, but with limited time and resources to produce advertisements and their very finite lives the adoption of tried and broadly acceptable themes, styles and methods becomes the most effective procedure until some more radical departure is undertaken. In turn, the broad conformity of the advertisements (and indeed marketing strategies) of products within a product class attest both to the workings of this principle and (presumably) its acceptance among recipients, otherwise the findings from routine market research in these product classes would lead to greater changes in advertising tactics. Nevertheless, the perception of advertisers about the nature and effectiveness of their advertising does exhibit remarkable variability; some retain essentially the same advertising themes (even the same advertisement) through extensive periods, thereby favouring one tactic for securing awareness (for instance), diametrically opposed to the alternative view which seeks awareness through change, even where the majority of the audience is the same in each case. In such instances the discriminating factor may be the extent to which a style of advertisement becomes essentially a part of the product itself. In other cases competitors use only marginally different-iated themes, for instance, celebrity endorsements, humour, sex, cartoon character, etc., either deliberately — to match a perceived competitor advantage, or coincidentally — arising from shared perceptions, similar research basis or a form of cultural convergence.

The variety of advertiser behaviour in the use of copy, media and in phasing, timing, and so on is a reflection of the perceptions and styles of advertisers and their advisers. Whilst the advertiser retains ultimate control, he may be influenced by or indeed dependent on the specialist advice of agency inter-mediaries. To this extent, advertisements may be regarded as a joint creation of the advertiser and his agency, though the composition of the firm's final 'product' in terms of the inputs from both sides is the outcome of a process of negotiation and selection between alternatives. Nevertheless, many advertise-ment styles come to be regarded as the distinctive product of certain agencies and their associated staff rather than of advertisers themselves (Crozier[39] and Channon[40]). On this basis the agency is effectively marketing its own product and providing a conspicuous, if superficial, view of its capabilities, which is helpful to the advertiser in his choice of agency. The attributes of an advertising style inevitably reflect the assumptions and intentions of the producers and these are as much a part of the product as the more conspicuous elements of the advertisement. In the marketing of advertising a communicable belief in the way advertising works is inextricably part of the agency's product. But it is hardly surprising that such beliefs, fashioned to the requirements or credulity of advertisers in their negotiations about style and portrayal, should not be seen as 'scientific' explanations of how advertising actually does work. In some cases these beliefs are explicit (e.g. Ogilvy[41] and Reeves,[42] quoted in Joyce[43]) but advertisements and campaigns can frequently sustain alternative rationales and be consistent with often opposing systems of beliefs. The advertiser himself, however, can only accept a belief and work in accord with it on the basis that most of his recipients will conform to the patterns of perception and behaviour consistent with that belief. Yet, in the nature of the purchasing of advertising, that belief need never (and probably for defensive reasons will not) be explicit and certainly it will not be formally tested. Thus it is part of the marketing of advertising itself that confrontation with the fundamentals of advertisers' beliefs should not occur and in this regard the arts of the negotiator are pre-eminent in judging the nature of and influencing his buyers' view, or implanting an alternative set of beliefs so that acceptance and confidence may be retained. Of course any demonstration of the apparent effects of particular advertisements or campaigns advances the seller's case. Further, it is a reflection of the competitive process at work that a succession of ideas, rationales, theories, research reports, case studies, methods and arguments to these ends must continually arise, to emulate the marketing pressures to which the advertisements themselves refer both as a means of neutralising the competitive advantages gained by others and to achieve greater efficiency and profit. In the somewhat claustrophobic advertising community, the balance of competitive advantage is comparatively easily disturbed and security, credibility and confidence difficult to maintain. The turnover of accounts at agencies themselves and the reasons, or rather the essential lack of objective reasons for this, bear admirable testimony to this competition. (See Doyle, Corstjens and Michell.[44])

The subject of this competition is the promise of what might be achieved and what it is claimed has been achieved; as such, it is never totally specified at any time. The advertising product is an intangible involving confidence and a belief in creativity. For these reasons and the exigencies of the processes of negotiation, the idea of *optimal* advertising is inappropriate. Essentially, advertising is about achieving satisfactory outcomes, subjective rather than objective optima, since restrictions of time, search and creativity, in conjunction with budget limitations, constrain advertisers and the agencies to the 'acceptable' and the 'better' rather than the 'best'.

The determination of appropriate advertising is the result of discovery; mistakes occur and lessons are learned and a consolidated view of advertising practice emerges and evolves. For products in the competitive situation, the facts of consumer behaviour, market circumstances and the characteristics of competitors and their advertising limit the competitive options but, nevertheless, fundamentally different advertising strategies can be conceived. However, arising from the uncertainty which attends advertising, management (unless forced by adverse circumstances into taking dramatic action), will probably adopt the least-risk strategy which in most cases involves only marginal changes in the major characteristics of the current campaign. While in principle they could change copy, media, total expenditure, agency, etc., selective action on one or two aspects is more likely, with a change in copy alone perhaps the most frequent outcome — reflecting views on advertising wear-out (see Rees,[45] Corkindale and Newall[46]).

Specialisation by function within firms may be inimical to the recognition of advertising as an entrepreneurial activity. In the face of uncertainty, the allocation of the resources to advertising will always be susceptible to challenge against the claims of more certain expenditures. Nevertheless, the advertising expenditure statistics recently revealed that even in recession (or perhaps as a direct result thereof), advertising allocations are generally maintained or increased. This in itself is a reflection of the lack of a mechanistic interpretation of the affordable, competitive parity and percentage of sales methods, though whether it reflects pursuit of specified objectives or is the outcome of a defensive or purposeful attitude is uncertain.

The complexity of advertising leads naturally to a large number of measurement possibilities; some aspects relating particularly to copy and media measurement and their use are considered here. Examples of the former include the characteristics of advertisements themselves and the effects of advertising in physiological, mental and behavioural terms, whilst the latter include vehicle and advertising exposure, readership assessment and the determination of audience characteristics. This measurement of advertising's features is primarily to aid management decisions, but different measures contribute variously to a given decision and some decisions are ill-served by any available measurement. In short, the choice between measures and the matching of these to requirements is not straightforward; indeed practitioners differ widely in their use of such measures with some forgoing whole areas of research which hold a pivotal role for others. To understand this variety it is necessary to consider in greater detail the efficacy of measurement and research.

Measurement, in general, is concerned with the assignment of numbers, according to some pre-selected set of rules, to those aspects which it is desired to measure. The presence of many features or systems of enumeration with different properties and attributes leads to a choice of measures in both technical and functional dimensions. The efficacy of measurement, however, depends on the selection of an appropriate rule and its correspondence with the purpose of measurement, the consistent and correct application of the chosen rule, and the reliability and validity of the measure. Efficacy is a matter of demonstration and critical acceptance; it does not necessarily follow from its intended adoption and utilisation. Measurement contributes to practical advertising decisions in a variety of ways which make different demands on the selection of the appropriate set of rules. The selection of the 'best' advertisement from a set of existing alternatives against a single pre-assigned criterion requires merely a rule to correspond to the criterion. This is less demanding than employing measurement to conceptualise the nature of 'best', the set of alternatives, and the criteria of choice. In the first case it is implied that there is correspondence between the rule, the purpose and the criterion, whereas in the latter any relationships must still be established. The possibility of multiple measures of a single criterion and of multiple criteria makes any correspondence harder to achieve and this is the general situation, for few advertising decisions can be legitimately conceived in terms of a sole criterion. Although superficially comparison may be expressed in terms of a single ordinal scale, the basis of this will usually be some combination of measures which in turn are the outcome of an acceptance of different rules and criteria.

Survey evidence of advertising practice reveals that single measure indicators of copy effectiveness and media characteristics are widely employed; in the latter case, opportunity to see and cost per thousand are prevalent whilst for comparative purposes and to aid the creation of copy the dominant measures employed by both advertisers and agencies relate to recall and attitude. (See Young[47] and Ostlund, Clancy and Sapra.[48]) Such measures facilitate the assessment of expectations and performance when these are specified strictly in terms of such measures, but although appropriate use is widespread the recall measure in particular is employed frankly as a surrogate, and often less precisely as a measure of awareness and exposure. A consideration which again raises the question of the underlying mechanism by which advertising 'works' and of the conceptualisation of the advertising process. Is awareness or exposure the initial step in a hierarchy of effects of mental activities or does it precede, without significant cognitive implications, or follow behaviour?

If the cognitive process model were to be preferred then the affective dimension of attitude becomes instrumental in causing a change of behaviour (*pace* Ray[49]). According to this model, because awareness is a necessary precursor of attitudinal change then a positive correlation between the dominant attitude and recall measures is suggested. On the other hand, the separation of affective and cognitive dimensions in this model would suggest that attitude and recall measures give different indications of the efficacy of given copy, precisely because what is specifically appropriate to gaining awareness/attention/recall is inappropriate to affect feelings and disposition. Negative correlations between these measures are frequently found (see Haskins[50] and Aaker and Day[51]) which suggest that indeed different aspects of advertising effectiveness are involved, thus requiring discrimination in the choice of measures. But even exemplary performances against such measures in appropriate contexts secures only intermediate objectives which are uncertainly related to eventual behavioural outcomes, and in the case of attitude measures may reflect behaviour rather than predict it. A possibility which finds support from such disparate explanations as those stemming from cognitive dissonance theorists, the behaviourists (see Chapter 4) and the empirical patterns assembled by Ehrenberg.[52] If both awareness and attitude — via the mechanism of behavioural intention — are routinely highly correlated with current usage and stem from it, as Ehrenberg demonstrates, then only in the case of the advertising of new products where previous behaviour is absent is either measure indicative of advertising's efficacy in communication, whilst even then its effects on behaviour remain uncertain. If in general the advertising of established brands has recall and attitude measures of effectiveness exhibiting negative correlation but both are positively related to behaviour, then the indications for management are confused. It is accordingly significant that the surveys referred to above found little interest amongst advertisers and agencies to measure and assess the inherent validity and reliability of the measures employed.

The conformity of brand advertising to a 'standard' appropriate to a product class is engendered by the common use of recall and attitudinal measures when these primarily reflect existing usage and a concomitant familiarity with the advertising for such brands. The measures so assiduously monitored remain sufficiently high only if this familiarity is maintained and, as such, the reassurance and reminder functions of advertising as a post-experience reinforcer are fused with the product into a broadened composite which both producers and consumers come to accept and expect. With the product class standard so determined the scope for copy alternatives is constrained and copy changes are likely to be only marginal in substance if not superficial in appearance. Given also the stability of consumption patterns and brand shares in the fast-moving consumer goods sector to which advertising primarily relates, the qualitative consistency of advertising is not surprising. The amount spent, the themes, the mechanisms for assessment and change are at any one time broadly predictable and as such industry stability is engendered.

5.6 Advertisers as competitors

Previous consideration, especially in Chapters 2 and 3, has been given to the economist's conceptions of competition and the role of advertisers. This section explores the role of advertising as a competitive device appropriate to the creation, maintenance and supplanting of competitive positions, where it is *assumed* that advertising is consistent with competition and is not inimical to it. In this usage, advertising arises from the desire or the necessity to compete: that is, advertising may be used aggressively or in defence of an existing situation. It is a property of ongoing competition where the competitive process is not naturally terminated at a specific date that the competitor must finely judge the merits and the risk of acting in a primarily defensive or aggressive mode; whether to maintain the status quo or to de-stabilise existing competition. In short, competitive businessmen have to distinguish the merits of rivalry and of co-existence and stability. That in fact they tend to the latter is the basic point underlying much of the economist's treatment of business behaviour from a theoretical perspective, but the tendency to eschew competition is also a potent factor in the way business is conducted, being to some minds an ultimately anti-social tendency which governmental policy may seek to redress (though competition regulations may derive from business lobbies). As Swann[53] puts it:

'For the plain truth is, and all experience points in this direction, that the all-pervading competition assumed to be a key ingredient in the free enterprise system would not survive long without anti-trust legislation. Historically, experience suggests that businessmen do not like competing . . . In an economy where there had been no significant competition policy there were few trades of any significance that did not exhibit instances of restrictive business practices, and in many industries restrictions were deeply entrenched. Further evidence of reluctance to compete is provided by the devices introduced to circumvent anti-trust laws . . . in the absence of anti-trust laws, the edge of competition will be significantly blunted.'

It is the reluctance to compete and the desire for stability which leads to the avoidance in most cases of the more overt forms of competition and especially of competition on the highly imitable basis of price concession. Accordingly, what price competition there is may take the form of surreptitious concessions or competition is pursued in ways which avoid price. It is this line of thought which conceives of advertising as a symptom of the lack of competition or the absence of a sufficiently vigorous desire to compete. Although advertising messages focused on price information and discounts, etc. would be a conspicuous exception, much advertising can be seen in one of two opposing ways: either as the expression of the desire to avoid price competition but to compete nevertheless, or as antithetical to competition. But for advertising to occur, *some* message actually must be transmitted and it is, ultimately, recipient response which determines the effect of advertisers' actions, whether this be competitive in intention or not. The message is designed with some form of recipient response in mind but the advertiser has no power to manipulate his audience who remain free agents in control of any decision they wish to make. If the response is inadequate it is the advertiser who must adapt: it is thus the characteristics of consumers and of the competitive conditions that fashion and determine the management of advertising. Of course the advertising is not without effects which in turn affect the reactions of all participants, but the advertiser at any one time is subservient to the situation rather than its creator.

The characteristics of the markets for those product classes and brands which are the most heavily and persistently advertised are themselves not subject to radical change; they routinely accommodate advertising without marked or sustained shifts in consumer purchasing patterns and, as seen above in the discussion of advertising determination, this stability in itself stabilises advertisers' behaviour. Advertising is, therefore, in the main cast in the defensive mode of competitive behaviour. The anodyne nature of much advertising (judged relative to the characteristics of its intended audience) is designed predominantly as a means of reassurance and to consolidate behaviour freely entered into, rather than to determine behaviour in ways which are not acceptable to the recipient. For both established and new products, the awareness–trial–reinforcement model[54] most succinctly and commensurately describes the competitive action of advertisers in response to the characteristics of market conditions. Where there is pre-existing choice and behaviour, product selection can only occur once awareness and some justification for action is conveyed. The cost-effective characteristics of advertising media lead competitors to the use of advertising both to create awareness of what is new and to reaffirm awareness and reinforce experience that has arisen from use. (If the previous experience is adverse, advertising is possibly counter productive, which tends to support the contention that advertised products can only survive if they are of higher quality than unadvertised products.) Of course the assurance about quality is not only derived from advertising — with retailers' own, often unadvertised, brands being a conspicuous case in point; moreover, exploitation of the presumed link between advertising and quality can be the basis for fraudulent trading which in turn encourages self-regulation in the advertising industry (see Chapter 1).

In addition to the minimal but essential conveying of awareness, the advertising message may define or suggest criteria or dimensions by which the product should be judged or perceived; these 'standards' again arise in response to the characteristics of recipients and competitive products. The attempt to convey exclusivity or prestige may be conducted with advertising — though sometimes advertising is thought inimical to this objective — in response to consumers' desires for such distinction, but more frequently the adequacy of the product and implied conformity for its users is the depicted standard.

The competitive process is enhanced and the revision of advertising copy is necessary when new features or products are developed. Where these product improvements are objectively slight and/or not readily discernible (even by experience), the advertising message, whether it consists of facts or association or whatever, can assume a greater role in the definition of the product and guide perception of both the objective and other features of the product to form a composite. The advertising recipient may purchase the product, but for repeat purchases to ensue — and these are the determinants of commercial success — the communicated composite must be appropriate to the consumer's experience of the product. If errors of judgement are made in the fashioning of such composites—and the vagaries of communication and the scale of media audiences make this likely—then a competitive position can be undermined. The advertising contribution to a composite or, more accurately, the set of perceived composites in a recipient audience can be substantial, but in itself it is insufficient. Whilst the advertising is 'free' and the product is bought, the composite must have commensurate value and any exaggerated claims/associations can prove counter productive if expectations on use exceed realisations. The competitive task of the advertiser is to match advertising to the product, its price and distributive features, and to the characteristics of the audience of existing and potential consumers. The co-ordination of the many components necessitated by this matching process, the level of ignorance of all pertinent considerations, and an uncertainty about the outcome—even with pre-testing and monitoring—render the advertising decision essentially entrepreneurial. Advertising alone cannot determine a product's success; the proportion of product failures (variously quoted in excess of one in two) usually with advertising support professionally conducted provides testimony to this. In some product circumstances, success is achievable without advertising; in other cases inadequate advertising can precipitate failure. The determinants of these varied cases are neither known with precision nor are they unchanging. Accordingly, advertising competition proceeds by imagination, trial and discovery, whose path is marked by both successes and failures.

5.7 Advertisers and the media

There is a symbiosis between advertisers and the media; the media are able to raise revenue from the sale of space/time and the advertiser is able to reach a broadly determinable audience. This joint dependence is not total, however; some media can and do exist without, or with only little, advertising (respectively books and certain magazines/journals) and the relative attraction of both parties is dependent on the size of the audience, the costs incurred by that audience and the rates charged to the advertisers, whilst the conditions of acceptance of advertising and the content of the medium are also significant. There is competition in both the provision and purchase of space and time in the media; the apportioning of the space/time is the outcome of the independent pursuit of the interests of the two sides working through a price and information mechanism. The degree of flexibility in determining the physical supply of space or time varies between media. The advertisement content per viewing hour is limited on British commercial television for instance, but with the introduction of the new station, Channel 4, there was a significant increase in sanctioned time. The availability of radio time has increased dramatically as well, from the era when Radio Luxembourg was the sole source, through the time of pirate stations to, most recently, legitimate commercial stations. In the print media, the number and lengths of publications are adjustable to market conditions and the advent of free sheets has provided a 'new' product offering variety in the mix between advertisements and editorial material. Whilst the price mechanism will broadly determine the relative advertising rates of the different media, in common with other markets the degree of concentration or exercise of market power by media owners (or, on occasion, large advertisers) is also relevant.

There is a certain irony in the traditional economic view of advertising being a symptom of monopoly power whilst the advertiser is himself the potential sufferer of monopoly pricing by the media owner; in this analysis there is redistribution from consumers to the media rather than just to the advertiser. In this regard, the profitability of the various media becomes the focus of interest and considerable variation is exhibited. At one pole, the fortunes of independent television companies whose viewers are not charged are predominantly dependent on the sale of time (and programmes), and the cost-effectiveness of such time even at 'high' prices has enabled these companies to achieve programming 'quality', to maintain sizeable audiences and to achieve high profits which in turn has attracted a governmental levy. At the other extreme, the lack of advertiser appeal stemming from high rates, insufficient audience or both has led to the closure of many publications, both magazines and newspapers, and indeed for the majority of media the relationship between cover charge, advertising rates and content can lead to fluctuating fortunes. The situation is further complicated because sustained profitability of particular media may not be necessary for their continued existence. Thus *The Times*, though constantly loss-making, is a successful *advertising* medium whose lack of profitability is due to other aspects of publishing, but it is nevertheless maintained primarily for non-commercial reasons. Many other publications involve elements of cross-subsidisation which permit some discretion in the setting of both cover prices and advertising rates.

5.8 Conclusions

A number of factors relating to the nature and context of advertising decision-making has impeded the development of a powerful theoretical rationale for the improved conduct of advertising. The complexity of advertising, arising from the nuances of communication, the immense variety of advertisements and the combinations of circumstances in which they are received, frustrates attempts at even rudimentary classification and frequently the categorisation of advertising leads merely to confusion, as additional dimensions impose qualification to the improved order. But the very features which pose such difficulties for theoreticians provide great scope for variety in the practice of advertising; moreover, in the absence of a unified theoretical understanding of the relevant dimensions of advertising, the scope for independent and individualistic assumptions about both advertising's effects and its conduct can flourish. This fertility finds many means of expression: in the composition of the marketing mix where advertising can be both complementary to, and in some degree a substitute for, other elements of the mix; in media selection and the timing and phasing of a campaign; in the creation and form of copy; in the selection and use of measurement; in the processes of negotiation, evaluation and judgement that advertising involves and in the formulation of objectives. Only selected aspects of advertising, however, are amenable to quantification but the reality of funding advertising expenditure naturally raises the issue of the cost-effectiveness of advertising in relation to sales and/or profit objectives. However, advertisers have had to adapt to the perennial difficulties of assessing advertising to the levels of accuracy comparable with other inherently uncertain expenditure. Nevertheless the desirability — the necessity even — to advertise, allied to the need for conviction in its conduct, and its very conspicuousness, ensure that exacting standards, primarily of a subjective form, must be met. The evolution of agencies, the movement of accounts between them, the quest for creativity in the themes and presentation of advertising and the varied use of media amply demonstrate the desire for improvement which, in turn, is the concomitant of a competitive process.

The role and significance of advertising differs for the various parties involved in this competition. Advertisers, media owners and advertising recipients all have other concerns which temper their dependence on advertising, though to various degrees. Agencies are more specialised and accordingly more dependent; for them the forces of competition are most exacting and as inter-mediaries they are susceptible to the actions of advertisers and media. But they are also dependent on the credibility and good name of advertising and act as an intermediary too between the authorities and advertising recipients, con-sumers and other producers. This centrality is significant to the conduct and nature of advertising; it is a means for avoiding extremes, indeed the charge of blandness often levelled against advertising may be due to this moderating effect, but also the tendency towards a common sub-culture amongst agencies and major advertisers does lead to some patterning of behaviour. However, it is also an intrinsic part of the maintenance of advertising standards. Whilst advertising must be of value to the advertiser, it depends for any effect on its acceptability which for responsible parties defines a common interest between producer, agency, media and the public. It is surely significant that arguments to support the view that there is an excessive amount of manipulative advertising and an effective conspiracy amongst advertisers overlook the role of the agency and media as intermediaries and attribute both an exaggerated influence to advertising and a corresponding low level of discernment to consumers.

References

1. Leone, R. P. and Schultz, R. L., 'A Study of Marketing Generalisations', *Journal of Marketing*, Vol. 44, Winter 1980, pp.10–18.
2. Colley, R. H., *Defining Advertising Goals for Measured Advertising Results*, New York: Association of National Advertisers, 1961, pp.62–68.
3. Corkindale, D. R. and Kennedy, S. H., *Measuring the Effect of Adver-tising*, Farnborough: Saxon House, 1975, p.154.
4. Lavidge, R. J. and Steiner, G. A., 'A Model for Predictive Measurements of Advertising Effectiveness', *Journal of Marketing*, Vol. 25, No. 4, 1961, pp.59–62.
5. Majaro, S., 'Advertising by Objectives', *Management Today*, January 1970, pp.71–73.
6. Colley, *op.cit.*
7. Taplin, W., 'Advertising Appropriation Policy', *Economica*, Vol. 26, 1959.
8. Rees, R. D., 'Advertising Budgeting and Appraisal in Practice', *Research Studies in Advertising*, No. 11, 1980, London: The Advertising Associa-tion.
9. Augustine, A. J. and Foley, W. F., 'How Large Advertisers set Budgets', *Journal of Advertising Research*, 15 (Oct. 1975), pp.11–20.
10. Printers' Ink, 'Ad Budgets: A Growing Science', *Printers' Ink*, December 16 1960, pp.16–27.
11. Patti, C. H. and Blasko, V., 'Budgeting Practices of Big Advertisers', *Journal of Advertising Research*, Vol. 4, No. 6, Dec. 1981, pp.23–29.
12. Rees, *op.cit.*

13. Rasmussen, A., 'The Determination of Advertising Expenditure', *Journal of Marketing*, 16, April 1952, pp.439–446.
14. Dorfman, R. and Steiner, P. O., 'Optimal Advertising and Optimal Quality', *American Economic Review*, Vol. 44, 1954, pp.826–836.
15. Nerlove, M. and Arrow, K., 'Optimal Advertising under Dynamic Conditions', *Economica*, Vol. 29, May 1962, pp.129–42.
16. Schmalensee, R., *The economics of Advertising*, Amsterdam: North Holland Publishing Company, 1972.
17. Cowling, K., Cable, J., Kelly, M. and McGuinness, T., *Advertising and Economic Behaviour*, London: Macmillan, 1975.
18. Peel, D. A., 'The Non-Uniqueness of the Dorfman-Steiner Condition: A Note', *Economica*, Vol. 40, 1973.
19. Lambin, J. J., 'Optimal Allocation of Competitive Marketing Efforts: An Empirical Study', *Journal of Business*, 43, Oct. 1970, pp.468–484.
20. Dorfman and Steiner, *op.cit.*, p.836.
21. Dhalla, N. K., 'Assessing the Long-term Value of Advertising', *Harvard Business Review*, Jan./Feb. 1978, pp.87–95.
22. *Broadbent, S., 'Price and Advertising: Volume and Profit', Admap*, Nov. 1980, pp.532–540
23. Schmalensee, *op. cit.*
24. Boyer, K. D., 'Information and Goodwill Advertising', *Review of Economics and Statistics*, Vol. 56, 1974, pp.541–548.
25. Porter, M. E., 'Consumer Behaviour, Retailer Power and Market Performance in Consumer Goods Industries', *The Review of Economics and Statistics*, Nov. 1974, pp.419–436.
26. Nerlove and Arrow, *op.cit.*
27. Nerlove and Arrow, *op.cit.*, p.130.
28. Koutsoyiannis, A., *Non Price Decisions*, London: Macmillan, 1982, pp.113–14.
29. Palda, K. S., *The Measurement of Cumulative Advertising Effects*, Englewood Cliffs, N.J.: Prentice-Hall, 1964.
30. Schmalensee, *op.cit.*, pp.12–13.
31. Clarke, D. G., 'Econometric Measurement of the Duration of Advertising Effect on Sales', *Journal of Marketing Research*, Vol. 13, November 1976, pp.345–357.
32. Weiss, D. L. and Windal, P. M., 'Testing Cumulative Advertising Effects: A comment on Methodology', *Journal of Marketing Research*, Vol. 17, August 1980, pp.371–378.
33. Clarke, *op.cit.*
34. Weiss and Windal, *op.cit.*
35. Scheidell, J. M., *Advertising, Prices and Consumer Reaction: A Dynamic Analysis*, Washington D.C.: American Enterprise Institute for Public Policy Research, 1978, p.55.
36. Scheidell, *ibid.*, p.17.
37. Schmalensee, *op.cit.*
38. Broadbent, *op.cit.*

39. Crozier, K., 'Puzzle Advertising' in Flood, P. R., Grant, C. L., O'Driscoll, A. (eds.), *Marketing: Future Imperfect; Proceeding of the Marketing Education* Group, Vol. 1, July 1981, pp.311–329.

40. Channon, C., 'Agency Thinking and Agencies as Brand', *Admap*, March 1981, pp.116–121.

41. Ogilvy, D., *Confessions of an Advertising Man*, New York: Atheneum, 1964.

42. Reeves, R., *Reality in Advertising*, New York: Alfred A. Knopf Inc., 1968.

43. Joyce, T., *What do we know about how Advertising Works?*, London: J. Walter Thompson Co., 1967.

44. Doyle, P., Corstjens, M. and Michell, P., 'Signals of Vulnerability in Agency–Client Relations', *Journal of Marketing*, Vol. 44, Fall 1980, pp.18–23.

45. Rees, *op.cit.*

46. Corkindale, D. and Newall, J., 'Advertising Thresholds and Wearout', *European Journal of Marketing*, Vol. 12, No. 5, 1978, pp.327–378.

47. Young, S., 'Copy Testing: For What? For Whom?', *Paper* presented to Annual Conference of Advertising Research Foundation, New York, October 1977.

48. Ostlund, L. E., Clancy, K. J. and Sapra, R., 'Inertia in copy Research, *Journal of Advertising Research*, Feb. 1980, pp.17–24.

49. Ray, M. L., 'Marketing Comunications and the Hierarchy of Effects', in Clarke, P. (ed.), New Models of Mass Communication Research, Vol. II, *Sage Annual Review of Communications Research*, Beverly Hills; Sage Publications Inc., 1973.

50. Haskins, J. B., 'Factual Recall as a Measure of Advertising Effectiveness', *Journal of Advertising Research*, March 1964, pp.2–8.

51. Aaker, D. A. and Day, G. S., 'A Dynamic Model of Relationships Among Advertising, Consumer Awareness, Attitudes and Behaviour', *Journal of Applied Psychology*, 59, 1974, pp.281–286.

52. Ehrenberg, A. S. C., 'Towards an Integrated Theory of Consumer Behaviour', *Journal of the Market Research Society*, Vol. II, No. 4, Oct. 1969, pp.306–323.

53. Swann, D., *Competition and Consumer Protection*, Harmondsworth: Penguin Books Ltd., 1979, pp.21–2.

54. Ehrenberg, 1974, *op.cit.*

6
Conclusions

The multi-disciplinary approach adopted in this book, together with the emphasis on the need to understand the realities as well as any theory of policy formation, has been intended to loosen the traditional hold of uni-disciplinary outlooks, to indicate the possibility of a less formally structured framework of analysis and to demonstrate the value of a more eclectic marshalling and assessment of our knowledge of advertising as it is relevant to the creation and implementation of public policy. It is ultimately necessary, however, to comprehend the whole area of policy as extra-disciplinary since the concerns of academic researchers and other investigators rarely coincide with those who make and effect policy. Economics, in particular, proceeds at a high level of abstraction, apparently necessitated by its adopted aim to seek a comprehensive understanding of advertising rather than to deal selectively and exclusively with its pathology. As a result, however, economists tend to scythe through the descriptive complexities of advertising and homogenize it in order to arrive at a handful of basic propositions which, despite the effort increasingly expended in empirical analysis, remain essentially theoretical. The conception of advertising in primarily quantitative (monetary) terms is to ignore the qualitative choices in the determination of copy, layout and media which are crucial determinants of advertising's effects. The assumption that these complex managerial decisions are optimised and lead to particular effects implies a determinism in human communication which is totally inappropriate. There is, moreover, an apparent desire to treat advertising within the structures (and strictures) of pre-existing theories of the firm and of consumer behaviour rather than to fashion theory to the unique characteristics peculiar to advertising. This leads to disparity between much theoretical analysis and the commonly observed features of advertisers and advertisements. There may be good theoretical reasons for some of this simplification, but theories devised with the narrow concern to meet the need for general prediction, which may be acceptable on this basis, are of extremely limited value in the resolution of policy-related issues; and this is nowhere more apparent than when empirical investigations of advertising depend so heavily upon the received theory that not only is much of the essential detail omitted, but also substantial determinants of advertising behaviour are excluded from analysis.

The behavioural science approach to the study of advertising's effects appears, by contrast, to exhibit a flexibility which is potentially of greater value to policy-makers, but with fragmented approaches there is, of course, no consensus. Thus, while hierarchy of effects information-processing models are comparatively well established, social psychologists and consumer researchers have not hesitated to pursue empirical investigations which have demonstrated that the posited sequence of mental events is generally improbable where consumer advertising is concerned and that attitudinal-behavioural consistency occurs only under stringently specified conditions of situational correspondence. Behavioural scientists have also investigated sources of communication and influence other than advertising and produced evidence for the view that the primarily effective sources are buyer- rather than marketer-dominated. Findings such as these, whilst having ramifications for advertising practice, certainly deserve to be taken more fully into account in both academic research into the effects and effectiveness of advertising and in the devising of public policy. Recognition of the variety of the effects of marketing communications and the necessity of closely observing the substance and context of advertising demonstrate the misleading nature of generalisation. But this marks only the beginning of a more realistic analysis of advertising. Demonstration of the comparatively weak capacity of advertising to determine thought and action (despite strident claims to the contrary) and recognition of its basic complementary role to other marketing instruments provides a needed focus for theoretical development and relevant empirical study, but considerable problems of identifying and isolating the effects of advertising remain.

However, the behavioural sciences, such as they are, elucidate important aspects of the actions of producers as well as consumers. Advertisers themselves respond to their perceptions of the effects and effectiveness of advertising, the general competitive context and their conceptualisation of the way advertising relates to other marketing elements in the firm's mix and to their target audiences. Advertisers vary in their use of all aspects of the mechanics of advertising; in terms of media, duration, size, frequency, etc. and even more conspicuously in the creative and qualitative dimensions of advertising. The creation and selection of appropriate advertisements, however, cannot be understood simply in terms of the close matching of particular components of advertisements to target audiences in conformity with a unified view of how advertising works, because creation and selection are diffused activities involving many participants with unco-ordinated views, each confronted by immense uncertainties of who will be reached, under what conditions and with what effect. Advertising is essentially a sequential process of creative discovery, of finding messages and modes of delivery mutually acceptable to both advertiser and audience, but because of the vagaries of human perception there will be what are variously judged to be conspicuous successes and failures. Nevertheless, on the basis of cumulating experience, certain established but not immutable practices arise sustained by appropriate rationales. Whatever uniformities may be discerned in the nature and pattern of advertising are explicable in these terms, but the ever evolving form both of advertisements and of the competitive organisational structure of advertising and the client industries which fashion them, attests to the essential experimental character of this means of communication. Also the shifting composition of the symbioses between advertiser and media and between these and recipients should be understood in such terms.

The volume of advertising, especially in the case of frequently-purchased consumer goods, depends on its association with branding and the competition both within and between product classes and different distributors. Consumers' low involvement both with advertising and the products to which it relates necessitates large rather than small volumes of advertising and its function is largely behavioural reinforcement, though its ability to communicate awareness may prompt the initial trial of a product.

The longevity of advertising as a discretionary means of communicating indicates its general cultural acceptance and credibility with recipients but experience also shows that its very amenability and acceptability can lead to both deliberate and unwilling abuse which present quite different problems of prevention and redress.

Recognition that the freedom to advertise entails an associated responsibility which is distributed between advertiser, agency and medium suggests that many of the various possible forms of abuse can be combatted by a greater exercise of this responsibility, encouraged by a process of increased awareness, education and the policing of industry codes of practice. The recent history of such a system in the UK shows that the industry can both create and enforce a code which maintains broadly acceptable standards, as far as can be judged from the typically small proportion of complaints made to the Advertising Standards Authority and from the judgement of its independent membership. The proportion of complaints per annum is typically a few thousand (less than 10,000) in relation to perhaps 15–25 *million* advertisements. Of course, prevention of any abuse and its consequent harm is to be preferred but the volume of advertising makes the vetting of *all* advertisements a practical impossibility. (The preliminary vetting of radio and television commercials by the Independent Broadcasting Authority is, at least at present, a more tractable undertaking; despite its code a small number of complaints are received though few are sustained.) Nevertheless, the scrutiny of advertisements in those product categories which provide the greatest level of complaint or which present novel forms of potential abuse does lead to revisions and extension of the code and thus by successive stages to a diminution of malpractice.

The responsiveness of the self-regulatory system to the concern expressed about previous standards and procedures has confounded many critics and surely led to a general improvement in the standard of advertisements. The likelihood that even with comprehensive vetting and assiduous monitoring of all advertisements there would still be controversy and complaint (arising from the expression of vested interests, affront to the often tiny minority with un-representatively susceptible tastes and ideologues), should not lead to complacency. (For a recent survey of public opinion concerning advertising see Appendix 4.) On the other hand, the standards which are employed to judge advertisements should not be significantly different from those applicable to other means and forms of communication and influence. It is, of course, a fact that most of these comparable aspects are not subject to any procedural control at all but like advertising are not exempt from a range of general laws which necessarily apply to what is actually illegal rather than just objectionable, taste-less, obnoxious or the cause of some form of offence.

The law is ultimately responsive to public opinion, but in respect of advertising there is no general clamour for change and there is also considerable scepticism of the law's role in any extension of advertising control; moreover, with regard to existing media the major precedents have probably been set. The reluctance of the law to embroil itself in often slight, publicity-inspired or petty issues deriving from the avarice of producers or the gullibility and inadequacy of consumers has led to a focus of legal attention on the more serious or blatantly criminal forms of abuse. For the other relatively minor cases, the inherent features and the realities of the administration of legal processes have made them generally inappropriate especially where there is uncertainty as to the outcome, and the time, effort and cost of such action is incommensurate with the offence.

The self-regulatory system and the legal domain are concerned primarily with the qualitative aspects of advertising, but policy issues arise in connection with the amount of advertising expenditure, the volume of advertising and its distribution between advertisers, products and media. These more generally quantitative aspects are foremost in the conventional economic analyses of advertising and with policy measures which have an economics rationale. The concern of critics has been with advertising in terms of monopoly power, the effect on prices, the possibility of a waste of resources, etc. and this has impelled (though not exclusively), such policy proposals as the selective or total ban on advertising, central regulation, counter-advertising funded by public funds, corrective advertising at the advertiser's expense, and a tax on advertising. Policy prescriptions that aim to reduce the incentive to advertise and to neutralise its effects are both more comprehensive and radical than the evolutionary approach and fine tuning associated with qualitative self-regulation, and derive principally from a particular conception of competition.

The critique of the prevailing concept of competition and competition policy in the light of the economic analysis that generally underpins it, and the wider consideration of consumer and producer behaviour given in our study do not, however, support the monolithic conclusions of traditional economic enquiry. Thus, the inevitable identification of advertising as both symbol and symptom of economic power and a concomitant belief in its *anti*-competitive role with determinate effects on prices, concentration, etc. is discounted in favour of an alternative view where a variety of outcomes is to be expected as a result of the inherent heterogeneity of advertising, the mode and manner of its use and the contexts in which it operates.

The alternative interpretation posits advertising as a competitive device associated with other elements of the marketing mix, co-existing on occasions with failure as well as commercial success and without pre-determinable and certain effects. It recognises the importance of individual perceptions, decision-making, time and circumstances on the outcome of aggregate behaviour and is consistent with the notion of a process of competition.

It is in the elucidation of the nature of this process of competition and the behaviour of the various participants — whether they be active or passive — that the major challenge to disciplinary enquiry arises. At present, only modest advances have been made probably because of the self-imposed rigidities of disciplinary definitions and procedures. This is perhaps most marked in the case of traditional microeconomics where the model of perfect competition continues to colour perceptions of market behaviour. In this respect, the insights of the Austrian school are particularly important in bringing the principles of economics to bear on the perceived realities of actual behaviour. But the economic framework, though valuable in itself, is neither comprehensive nor in a practitioner's sense operational. Indeed, the economist's approach to advertising has often been thought of as 'academic' which is also an euphemism for irrelevant. But operational significance is neither necessary for a discipline nor the intention of economists, though their theorising and empirical assessments must be consonant with actual behaviour if the results are to be credible. Accordingly, there must be greater recognition of the role of advertising, the processes of its creation and organisation as it involves advertisers, distributors, agencies and media and of the variety of audiences who encounter and utilise advertising in so many different ways. The adoption of a transaction view of advertising which is compatible with both an economics and a marketing approach is the most productive line of enquiry, but this requires a highly disaggregated mode of analysis of both the consumer and producers. Furthermore, it is necessary to recognise the role of entrepreneurship in advertising, for the skills of creativity and alertness are constantly required given the ephemeral lives of advertisements and the changing contexts, composition and perceptions of audiences on the one hand and the competitive environment — of innumerable advertisements and products — on the other, for decisions are rarely routine nor information adequate. Again, the disregard that traditional economics accords to entrepreneurial function contributes to its limitations in the analysis of advertising and in this regard the Austrian view is particularly apposite.

The Austrian approach, despite the esoteric nature of its conceptualisations and economics focus, does have many complementary features to marketing which earlier chapters have indicated. However, it is the nature of disciplines, both economics and marketing, to develop and employ concepts in a specialised — even insular — fashion. Moreover, a certain complementarity does not imply uniformity and there are indeed many interesting problems which merit further consideration and whose resolution is necessary before progress in understanding can be made on a multi-disciplinary or unified front. The formulation of such problems is clearly inappropriate here but, in keeping with the attention given at various stages in this book to a number of dichotomies including objectivity and subjectivity, behaviourism and mentalism, individualism and collectivism, information and persuasion, the examination of what at first sight might appear to be an inconsistency is warranted. The discussion of mentalism and behaviourism led to our favouring the latter as a more convincing and appropriate view, at least for the advertising of those frequently-bought brands in established product classes, but the merits of the subjectivist treatment of advertising in individualistic terms, which we also favour, would seem to be more consistent with a mental process view. Moreover, the limitations imposed on aggregation by the adoption of a subjectivist approach would seem to impede the aggregate analysis that is necessary if advertisers are to act in accord with a behaviouristic interpretation.

That the inconsistencies are more apparent than real derives from the different purposes to which the delineation of constructs are particularly suited and to the constraints of purely disciplinary perspectives. These matters may be demonstrated in the practical, if pragmatic, context of producer behaviour. If the advertiser believes that advertising has a potentially unique effect on each individual exposed to it, an effect which is ultimately knowable only to the individual himself and as such is both unobservable and non-aggregatable, he views advertising in subjectivist terms; but, nevertheless, if he must administer advertising then the available objective indicators of any advertising effects on recipients, of both a qualitative and quantitative nature, may be helpful. But such are the many and diverse influences on recipient behaviour, in addition to the probably slight effect of advertising, and such is the necessity to consider the effect of advertising on the totality of the market situation that any pursuit of the rich detail which is implicit in the subjectivist approach, must be forsaken in favour of a more crude, but aggregate behaviouristic approach providing this is a valid generalisation of individuals' behaviours. In advertising the scope for comprehensive description in objective terms, especially within the time periods that decisions must be made, ensures however that subjective considerations are highly relevant both to the perceptions of advertiser and, of course, to the recipients. Whilst in the short term there need be no correspondence between those sets of perceptions, with competition providing alternatives and trial or re-trial providing experience, any substantial mismatch cannot be sustained.

The rigours of competing, however, can lead some to eschew competition and by collusive activity or matched responses to attempt to transform an otherwise competitive situation into a form of static posturing. Advertising is frequently associated with such a role, but whilst advertising can be deployed defensively it is difficult to understand how active and continuing communication with an audience can be consistent with the avoidance of competition. Advertising by itself is insufficient to guarantee stability; it may attempt to reinforce existing behaviour and foster awareness of product existence, but the periodic changes in copy and the product development process which is closely allied to it are essentially de-stabilising. They encourage a re-appraisal of (perhaps habitual) behaviour which is intended to confirm product acceptance by its existing users and encourage trial and re-trial by others. Moreover, with the consumers' typical low involvement and the existence of acceptable alternatives in most product classes, the maintenance of stability is itself an exacting standard. Rather than the very existence of advertising being amenable to association with unproductive and unacceptable competition (a form of non-competition merely because there are no appreciable movements in the sales of an overall product class), the reinforcement, reminder and reassurance functions of advertising become a virtual necessity to individual producers. It is possible that these functions may be achieved by other means, but the cost-effectiveness of advertising, despite its limitations, has proved sufficiently and continuously persuasive to advertisers through eras which have exhibited a wide range of technically innovative and cultural features.

The anti-competitive association of advertising is more tenable in terms of entry prevention, but spending on advertising for this purpose is extremely speculative given its weak influence. Moreover, expenditure in excess of the requirements of cost-effective communication actually renders the advertiser more vulnerable, as the innumerable successful market penetrations employing advertising to *establish* and thereafter maintain a competitive position demonstrate.

Advertising then is a competitive device and many of its positive attributes and indeed defects can be understood in terms of competition: excesses of competitive zeal, misjudgements due to pressure of time or inadequate research, insensitivity, exploitation of a medium and consumers, are all sustainable charges in particular instances which have a clear relation to competition as a striving activity. Competition, as rivalry, is in most organised contexts conducted within a set of rules — perhaps formalised, often implicit; commercial competition including advertising is no exception. However, the discovery of the appropriate rules must stem from experience and be a gradual process of adjustment and re-adjustment. Competition itself has the power to eliminate some forms of excess and abuse but prevention is both more certain and immediate and obviates the need for redress. The practical difficulties, however, of conceiving and implementing a comprehensive scheme are formidable and, ultimately, potentially in conflict even with the benefits of competition. The scale of abuse or any negative effects of advertising do not warrant such a scheme. There is a place for some regulation but this is confined to the qualitative characteristics of advertising.

In the UK the self-regulatory system with, in principle, a three stage self vetting by advertiser, agency and medium should be sufficient if the code of practice is comprehensive and the parties conscientious. This sufficiency, however, must be continually demonstrated. Nevertheless, in conclusion, we are impressed by the general social and commercial consensus regarding advertising. Advertising abuse is only a blemish, kept in check as much by the conspicuous competition amongst advertisers as by regulatory systems. Advertising is a thrusting medium; it seeks to be innovative so the policy issues that arise are typically reactive rather than proactive. The difficulties in either case in formulating and implementing policy are considerable. In influencing the climate of opinion and in illuminating particular topics we believe a variety of disciplinary approaches have much to contribute, but that their potential is still largely unrealised and could be enhanced if shibboleths are examined in a more inter-disciplinary spirit. It is hoped this book has made a modest contribution in this respect.

Appendix 1

Statutes and statutory instruments with special relevance to advertising and related trading practices

Accommodation Agencies Act 1953
Administration of Justice Act 1970
Administration of Justice Act 1977
Adoption Act 1976 (s. 58)
Betting, Gaming and Lotteries Act 1963 (ss. 10 and 22)
Building Societies Act 1962 (ss. 14, 51, 52, 57)
Business Advertisements (Disclosure) Order 1977
Cancer Act 1939 (s. 4)
Children Act 1958 (s. 37)
Civil Aviation (Licensing) Act 1960 (s. 7)
Civil Aviation (Aerial Advertising) Regulations 1971
Companies Act 1948 (ss. 50, 108)
Consumer Credit Act 1974 (and Regulations made thereunder)
Consumer Safety Act 1978
Consumer Transactions (Restrictions on Statements) Order 1976
Copyright Act 1956
Criminal Justice Act 1925 (s. 38)
Powers of Criminal Courts Act 1973
Customs and Excise Act 1952 (ss. 162 and 164) as amended by Finance Acts
 1964 (s. 2) and 1967 (s. 5)
Defamation Act 1952
Design Copyright Act 1968
Employment Agencies Act 1973 (and Regulations made thereunder)
Energy Act 1976 (s. 15)
Fair Employment (Northern Ireland) Act 1976
Fair Trading Act 1973
Finance Act 1965 (s. 15)
Food and Drugs Act 1955 (as subsequently amended) (and Regulations made
 thereunder)
Gaming Act 1968 (s. 42)

Geneva Convention Act 1957 (s. 6)

Hearing Aid Council Act 1968

Indecent Advertisements Act 1889

Independent Broadcasting Authority Act 1981

Insurance Companies Act 1974

Legal Aid Act 1974

London Cab Act 1968, as amended by London Cab Act 1973

Lotteries and Amusements Act 1976

Mail Order Transactions (Information) Order 1976

Marine, etc. Broadcasting (Offences) Act 1967

Medicines Act 1968 (and Regulations made thereunder)

Misrepresentation Act 1967

Control of Pollution Act 1974

Obscene Publications Act 1959

Obscene Publications Act 1964

Opticians Act 1958

Patents, etc. (International Conventions) Act 1938

Pharmacy and Poisons Act 1933

Post Office Act 1953 (ss. 61, 62, 63) and Fictitious Stamp Regulations 1937

Prevention of Fraud (Investments) Act 1958 (as amended)

Prices Act 1974 (and Regulations made thereunder)

Professions Supplementary to Medicine Act 1960

Protection of Depositors Act 1963

Race Relations Act 1976

Representation of the People Act 1983

Road Traffic Act 1979

Sale of Goods Act 1979

Sex Discrimination Act 1975

Sunday Observance Act 1780

Supply of Goods and Services Act 1982

Textile Products (Indications of Fibre Content) Regulations 1973

Theft Act 1968 (s. 23)

Town and Country Amenities Act 1974

Town and Country Planning Act 1971 (and Orders made thereunder —
    Control of Advertisements Regulations 1969)

Trade Descriptions Act 1968 (and Regulations made thereunder)

Trade Descriptions Act 1972

Trade Marks Act 1938

Trading Stamps Act 1964

Unsolicited Goods and Services Acts 1971 and 1975 (and Regulations and
    made thereunder)

Venereal Diseases Act 1917

Weights and Measures Act 1963 (and Regulations made thereunder) as
amended by the Weights and Measures Act 1979

Note: There are no statutory provisions dealing with tobacco advertising.
There is, however, a voluntary agreement between the tobacco manufacturers
and the Government covering such things as health warnings. Cigarette
advertisements must also comply with Appendix H of the British Code of
Advertising Practice. Advertisements for alcoholoc drinks are covered by
Appendix J of the Code.

Source: Appendix L British Code of Advertising Practice 1979.

Appendix 2

Proposal for a Council Directive relating to the approximation of the laws, regulations and administrative provisions of the Member States concerning misleading and unfair advertising

(Submitted by the Commission to the Council on 1 March 1978)

THE COUNCIL OF THE EUROPEAN COMMUNITIES

Having regard to the Treaty establishing the European Economic Community, and in particular Article 100 thereof,

Having regard to the proposal from the Commission,

Having regard to the opinion of the European Parliament,

Having regard to the opinion of the Economic and Social Committee,

Whereas the laws against misleading and unfair advertising now in force in the Member States differ widely; whereas, since advertising reaches to a large extent beyond the frontiers of individual Member States, it has a direct affect on the establishment and the functioning of the common market;

Whereas unfair and misleading advertising is likely to restrict the establishment of a system to ensure that competition is not distorted within the common market;

Whereas misleading and unfair advertising may cause a consumer to take decisions prejudicial to him when acquiring property or accepting services and the differences between the laws lead, in many cases, not only to inadequate levels of consumer protection, but also prevent the execution of advertising campaigns beyond national boundaries and thus affect the free circulation of goods and provision of services;

Whereas the preliminary programme of the European Economic Community for a consumer protection and information policy provides in particular for appropriate action for the protection of consumers against false or misleading advertising;

Whereas it is in the interest of the public in general, as well as that of consumers and all those who, in competition with one another, carry on a trade, business or profession, throughout the common market, to harmonize national provisions against misleading and unfair advertising;

Whereas minimum criteria for determining whether advertising is misleading or unfair should be established for this purpose;

Whereas, in view of modern techniques of communication, the definition of 'advertising' must be worded broadly, but should not extend to policy statements, the publication of comparative product tests by independent organizations and any similar statements;

Whereas the concepts of 'misleading advertising' and 'unfair advertising' must as far as possible be defined by reference to objective criteria;

Whereas comparative advertising may be beneficial to a consumer and a competitor to the extent that it compares material and verifiable details with each other and is neither misleading nor unfair;

Whereas the laws to be adopted by Member States against misleading and unfair advertising must be adequate and effective; whereas it is a matter for the Member States whether they wish these to be matters of civil law, administrative law or criminal law or a combination thereof;

Whereas persons affected, as well as associations with a legitimate interest in the matter, must have facilities for initiating proceedings against misleading or unfair advertising and in particular for obtaining the quick cessation of misleading or unfair advertisements;

Whereas if a person advertises by making a factual claim the burden of proof that his claim is correct must lie with him;

Whereas the provisions of this Directive do not preclude Member States from adopting other measures for the protection of consumers, subject to their obligations under the Treaty establishing the EEC and in particular the rules on the free movement of goods and services and competition,

HAS ADOPTED THIS DIRECTIVE:

Article 1

The objective of this Directive is to protect consumers, persons carrying on a trade, business or profession, and the interests of the public in general against unfair and misleading advertising.

Article 2

For the purpose of this Directive:
— 'advertising' means the making of any pronouncement in the course of a trade, business or profession for the purpose of promoting the supply of goods or services,

— 'misleading advertising' means any advertising which is entirely or partially false or which, having regard to its total effect, including its presentation misleads or is likely to mislead persons addressed or reached thereby, unless it could not reasonably be foreseen that these persons would be reached thereby,

— 'unfair advertising' means any advertising which:

   (a)   casts discredit on another person by improper reference to his nationality, origin, private life or good name, or

   (b)   injures or is likely to injure the commercial reputation of another person by false statements or defamatory comments concerning his firm, goods or services, or

   (c)   appeals to sentiments of fear, or promotes social or religious discrimination, or

   (d)   clearly infringes the principle of the social, economic and cultural equality of the sexes, or

   (e)   exploits the trust, credulity or lack of experience of a consumer, or influences or is likely to influence a consumer or the public in general in any other improper manner,

— 'goods' means property of any kind, whether movable or immovable, and any rights or obligations relating to property.

Article 3

1.   In determining whether advertising is misleading or unfair, pronounce-ments shall be taken into consideration concerning in particular:

(a)   the characteristics of the goods or services, such as nature, performance, composition, method and date of manufacture or provision, fitness for purpose, usability, quantity, quality, geographical or commercial origin, properties and the results to be expected from use;

(b)   the conditions of supply of the goods or services, such as value and price, conditions of contract and of guarantee;

(c)   the nature, attributes and rights of the advertiser, such as his identity, sol-vency, abilities, ownership of intellectual property rights or awards and distinctions.

2.   Advertising shall in particular be regarded as misleading when it omits material information, and, by reason of that omission, gives a false impression or arouses expectations which the advertiser cannot satisfy.

Article 4

Comparative advertising shall be allowed, as long as it compares material and verifiable details and is neither misleading nor unfair.

Article 5

Member States shall adopt adequate and effective laws against misleading and unfair advertising.

Such laws shall provide persons affected by misleading or unfair advertising, as well as associations with a legitimate interest in the matter, with quick, effec-tive and inexpensive facilities for initiating appropriate legal proceedings against misleading and unfair advertising.

Member States shall in particular ensure that:

— the courts are enabled, even without proof of fault or of actual prejudice:

   (a)   to order the prohibition or cessation of misleading or unfair adver-tising; and

(b)   to take such a decision under an accelerated procedure, with an interim
      or final effect;

— the courts are enabled:

(a)   to require publication of a corrective statement; and

(b)   to require publication of their decision either in full or in part and in
      such form as they may judge adequate;

— ensure that the sanctions for infringing these laws are a sufficient deterrent,
  and, where appropriate, take into account the financial outlay on the advertising, the extent of the damage and any profit resulting from the
  advertising.

Article 6

Where the advertiser makes a factual claim, the burden of proof that his claim
is correct shall lie with him.

Article 7

Where a Member State permits the operation of controls by self-regulatory
bodies for the purpose of counteracting misleading or unfair advertising, or
recognizes such controls, persons or associations having a right to take legal
proceedings under Article 5 shall have both that right and the right to refer the
matter to such self-regulatory bodies.

Article 8

The present Directive does not prevent Member States taking or maintaining
other measures for the protection of consumers against misleading or unfair
advertising to the extent that these measures are in conformity with the Treaty.

Article 9

Member States shall bring into force the measures necessary to comply with
this Directive within 18 months of its notification and shall forthwith inform
the Commission thereof.

Member States shall communicate to the Commission the text of the main provisions of national law which they adopt in the field covered by this Directive.

Article 10

This Directive is addressed to the Member States.

Source: Official Journal of the European Communities

Appendix 3

Amendment to the proposal for a Council Directive relating to the approximation of the laws, regulations and administrative provisions of the Member States concerning misleading and unfair advertising

(Submitted by the Commission to the Council pursuant to Article 149 (2) of the EEC Treaty on 10 July 1979)

ORIGINAL TEXT | AMENDED TEXT

Article 2

For the purpose of this Directive:

— 'Advertising' means the making of any pronouncement in the course of a trade, business or profession for the purpose of promoting the supply of goods or services,

— 'Misleading advertising' means any advertising which is entirely or partially false or which, having regard to its total effect, including its presentation, misleads or is likely to mislead persons addressed or reached thereby, unless it could not reasonably be foreseen that these persons would be reached thereby,

— 'Unfair advertising' means any advertising which:

   (a)   casts discredit on another person by improper reference to his nationality, origin, private life or good name; or

Article 2

For the purpose of this Directive:

— 'Advertising' means the making of a *representation in any form* in the course of a trade, business or profession for the purpose of promoting the supply of goods or services,

unchanged

— 'Unfair advertising' means any advertising which:

   (a)   casts discredit on another person by (*one word deleted*) reference to his nationality, origin, private life or good name; or

ORIGINAL TEXT	AMENDED TEXT

(b) injures or is likely to injure the commercial reputation of another person by false statements or defamatory comments concerning his firm, goods or services; or

(b) unchanged

(c) appeals to sentiments of fear, or promotes social or religious discrimination; or

(c) *abuses or unjustifiably arouses sentiments of fear;* or

(d) clearly infringes the principle of the social, economic and cultural equality of the sexes; or

(d) *promotes discrimination on grounds of sex, race or religion;* or

(e) exploits the trust, credulity or lack of experience of a consumer, or influences or is likely to influence a consumer or the public in general in any other improper manner;

(e) *abuses* the trust, credulity or lack of experience of a consumer, or influences or is likely to influence a consumer or the public in general in any other improper manner;

— 'Goods' means property of any kind, whether movable or immovable, and any rights or obligations relating to property.

unchanged

Article 3

1. In determining whether advertising is misleading or unfair, pronouncements shall be taken into consideration concerning in particular:

Article 3

1. In determining whether advertising is misleading or unfair, *representations* shall be taken into consideration concerning in particular: (English text only)

(a) the characteristics of the goods or services, such as nature, performance, composition, method and date of manufacture or provision, fitness for purpose, usability, quantity, quality, geographical or commercial origin, properties and the results to be expected from use;

unchanged

ORIGINAL TEXT	AMENDED TEXT

(b) the conditions of supply of the goods or services, such as value and price, conditions of contract and of guarantee;

unchanged

(c) the nature, attributes and rights of the advertiser, such as his identity, solvency, abilities, ownership of intellectual property rights or awards and distinctions.

unchanged

2.   Advertising shall in particular be regarded as misleading when it omits material information, and, by reason of that omission, gives a false impression or arouses expectations which the advertiser cannot satisfy.

2.   Advertising shall in particular be regarded as misleading when *it is not readily recognizable as an advertisement or* when it omits material information, and, by reason of that omission, gives a false impression or arouses *reasonable* expectations which the *advertised goods or services* cannot satisfy.

Article 5

Member States shall adopt adequate and effective laws against misleading and unfair advertising.

Such laws shall provide persons affected by misleading or unfair advertising, as well as associations with a legitimate interest in the matter, with quick, effective and inexpensive facilities for initiating appropriate legal proceedings against misleading and unfair advertising.

Article 5

Member States shall adopt adequate and effective laws against misleading and unfair advertising.

Such laws shall provide persons affected by misleading or unfair advertising as well as associations with a legitimate interest in the matter, with quick, effective and inexpensive facilities for *either*:

(*a*)   initiating appropriate legal proceedings against misleading or unfair advertising; or

(*b*)   *bringing the matter before an administrative authority with adequate powers.*

ORIGINAL TEXT	AMENDED TEXT
Member States shall in particular ensure that:	Member States shall in particular ensure that:
— the courts are enabled, even without proof of fault or of actual prejudice:	— the courts *or the administrative authority, as appropriate,* are enabled, even without proof of *intention or negligence or* of actual prejudice:
(a) to order the prohibition or cessation of misleading or unfair advertising; and	(a) to order the prohibition or cessation of misleading or unfair advertising; and
(b) to take such a decision under an accelerated procedure, with an interim or final effect,	(b) to take such a decision under an accelerated procedure, with an interim or final effect,
— the courts are enabled:	— the courts *or the administrative authority, as appropriate,* are enabled:
(a) to require publication of a corrective statement; and	(a) to require publication of a corrective statement; and
(b) to require publication of their decision either in full or in part and in such form as they may judge adequate;	(b) to require publication of their decision either in full or in part and in such form as they may judge adequate;
— the sanctions for infringing these laws are a sufficient deterrent, and, where appropriate, take into account the financial outlay on the advertising, the extent of the damage and any profit resulting from the advertising.	*Member States shall ensure that the consequences of infringing laws and decisions in the field of misleading and unfair advertising take into account the extent of the harm.*

ORIGINAL TEXT	AMENDED TEXT
	Where the abovementioned powers are entrusted to an administrative authority, the authority shall not be controlled by advertising interests, shall be obliged to give reasons for its decisions, and shall be under a duty to exercise its powers so as effectively to control misleading and unfair advertising; and procedures shall exist whereby improper exercise by the authority of its power or improper failure by the authority to exercise its powers or to apply reasonable standards can be reviewed by the courts at the request of the parties.

ORIGINAL TEXT — **AMENDED TEXT**

Article 6

Originally Article 7 — unchanged

Article 7

(Originally Article 6)

Article 6

Where the advertiser makes a factual claim, the burden of proof that his claim is correct shall lie with him.

Where the advertiser makes a factual claim, the burden of proof that his claim is correct shall *in civil and administrative proceedings* lie with him.

Article 9

Member States shall bring into force the measures necessary to comply with this Directive within 18 months of its notification and shall forthwith inform the Commission thereof.

Member States shall communicate to the Commission the text of the main provisions of national law which they adopt in the field covered by this Directive.

Article 9

Member States shall bring into force the measures necessary to comply with this Directive within 24 months of its notification and shall forthwith inform the Commission thereof.

Member States shall communicate to the Commission the text *of all provisions* of national law which they adopt in the field covered by this Directive.

Source: Official Journal of the European Communities

Appendix 4

Public Opinion and Advertising

This is a brief account of the findings of a 1980–81 survey of the opinion of a representative national sample of 1116 adults conducted by the Advertising Association[1] to assess public interest in and attitudes towards advertising.[2]

It was found that advertising as a *topic of conversation* in comparison with a wide range of domestic and national issues including religion, professional sport, trades unions, politicians, education, big business, clothing and fashion, government, family life, Civil Service and bringing up children was bracketed between the Civil Service and big business with a rating half that of religion and one third that of politicians with other aspects of the above claiming precedence. Four per cent of the sample held strong opinions of advertising — one half that regarding clothing and fashion — and whilst broadly comparable to opinion concerning big business and the Civil Service this was relatively small compared with most issues. As a topic that warranted *attention* and *change*, only two per cent cited advertising in comparison with three per cent for professional sport and religion, four per cent for big business and five per cent for family life. This broad indication of acceptance of, if little interest in, advertising is consistent with the further finding that 77 per cent expressed some measure of approval of advertising and with the proportion of those disliking advertising being 10 per cent in the case of newspapers and magazines and 15 per cent for television commercials.

Follow-up in depth study of the critics found these to have certain characteristics: a comparative lack of exposure to advertising, family centredness, political conservatism and anti-materialism. This in turn is compatible with their criticisms of advertising for portraying a stereotyped and unreal image of family life and extravagant products as everyday essentials. There was also evidence, however, that these opinions were projected to others whilst the respondents felt themselves personally to be unaffected by advertising and in any event its effects were felt to be a matter of personal responsibility both in regard to media exposure and in behavioural response to advertising. There was criticism of the perennially pervading themes of some advertisements, with sexism, silliness, tastelessness, triviality and patronising tone most prevalent, but detailed investigation found a tendency to translate objection to a product or advertiser to a criticism of advertising *per se*.

References

1. 'Public Attitudes to Advertising 1980/81', The Advertising Association, 1981.
2. For a summary of the full report see Coulson, D., 'Public Attitudes to Advertising', *Independent Broadcasting*, 31 March 1982, pp 7–10.

Index